# The South I Knew:
# Love Letters to My Children

# The South I Knew:
# Love Letters to My Children

Christian Monroe Holliday Douglas

Dedicated to my three beautiful children,
Holly, Russell, and David Jr.


I love y'all so much.
Listen to God and discover your talents.
Follow your hearts and passions.
Be good to yourselves.
Then you can do for others.

ISBN-13: 978-1499320794
ISBN-10: 1499320795

# CONTENTS

# PREFACE
## Reminisce, Recollect, and Write Down

Dear Holly, Russell, and David,

This is not a history book. These are my recollections of the South and the Galivants Ferry in which I grew up. Many are stories of our family members that have been passed down from one generation to another, written on old worn yellow stationery, found in old files as handwritten memos, old business transactions, personal letters between your relatives and non-relatives, and lots of family tales.

There are many other stories and records which are not about your family. The folks who lived in and around Galivants Ferry were and are our "kinfolk." My definition of "kinfolk" is not blood relatives, but in some cases they might have been; you probably have some living here today. Any way you choose to hear their stories, they are still your family. The old Southerners took care of each other. The families that still live here have, for the most part, been here for many generations, just like the Hollidays. If it had not been for them, we might not have survived for five generations in this one small township. At the least, things would have been very different. We would have been elsewhere – scattered in the wind.

In addition, I started taking pictures of the South I knew. I wanted to show y'all how and where I grew up. It wasn't all there. Barns, tenant homes, the old blacksmith shop and pack houses were being torn down or allowed to collapse. The general accepted reasoning behind all this was and is, "if it doesn't make money or produce a cash flow, tear it down." I saw very little emotion, if any, about tearing down these old buildings…our connections to the past. The South I knew was disappearing rapidly.

I know you can't hang on to everything, but you can preserve some. My parents were still alive and they still loved the memories, but as you get older, it's harder to hang onto the way you were raised. Your children and the world around you push you into accepting the 'new ways'. They make you feel old and antiquated, out of date. I am guilty of doing this to my father.

When I moved back home, fresh from a big city, I remember thinking, "These people are backwards. They have got to get with it." The first time I moved back there were no computers or tax ID numbers. Everything was filed in "shucks," which were old yellowed paper files, flimsy with notes in them as old as twenty years to remind 'so and so' to be sure and clean out that ditch, or cut the 60-year-old timber 'cause it was dying. I remember thinking, "they are in the dark ages; we have got to modernize."

Yes, we did need a few updates, but the more I looked back and before all these discoveries were made, I realized I was a young 'whippersnapper'. It sank in that you can move forward, but be careful, 'cause our fore fathers and elders were smarter and wiser than us in lots of areas. Compromise is essential, and the fact that I even had files to look into showed they were able to survive three generations in one place. Who was I to criticize?

There is a connective thread that holds your past, present, and future together. I am an open-minded woman and I have lived in other places, traveled, gone to school, worked various jobs, married twice and gave birth to the three of you. For some strong reasons, I wanted to come home. Your daddy also wanted to move to Galivants Ferry. It was a culture shock relocating back to the country from Greenville, SC, a rather large city, but I think you three are happy we made the transition. You got to know the roots of the Hollidays after having lived where your Douglas roots run deep. I'm glad you got to know your grandparents here.

Now, I want to tell you more about the past that desperately needs to be remembered, so you can convey these stories and memories to your children. That's how oral history has worked for thousands of years. In recent years, as technology and the need for instant results has taken over, we've tended as a people to forget about the power of oral storytelling. However, you are from the South, the cradle of storytelling – and nothing matters more to true Southerners than passing down their family traditions, stories and histories, which I am doing now.

The following stories are about your folks, way of life, social changes, and things that continue to disappear in the South I Knew. Not all stories have happy subjects or endings, but they are a part of history and had a huge impact on Galivants Ferry and me. I've included photographs of many people and ways of life which do not exist today, reading along of just how simple, beautiful and even magical the rural Southern lifestyle can be. It must be magical – look at how many great books and movies have featured Southern landscapes and people you know as your own. Times change, but we need to understand the past in order to go forward into the future.

There are genealogy charts of our "family trees," heritage and lineage which I want you to be aware, such as our direct link to King George and Charlemagne lines, and the Magna Carta, to name a few. These don't make you special, but they help illustrate your past. What you do with your God given life, talents, and purposes will determine your destiny.

The true purpose of this book is for y'all to feel the essence of the emotions, colorful characters of the South, and sentiments about your family roots, which I hold in my body and soul.

It's priceless. Enjoy the ride.

# PROLOGUE
## The South I Knew

All Southerners – especially the older ones – have a certain way of greeting someone new.

They want to know who you are, where you're from, who's your daddy, what's he do, where do you go to church, and so on. Or in some cases, it boils down to: *"Who are your people?"* They don't mean any harm; it's in their genes to want to know the details of your "whereabouts."

Now that doesn't mean that they will tell you about themselves. Don't get me wrong; this culture still exists today. Southerners, like other familial societies of the world, are a "tight knit" crowd. They love their roots even though they keep family secrets to themselves. They cherish their ancestors (maybe some more than others). Most wouldn't do a thing to hurt their family name. They are tight-lipped when it comes to their own affairs; however, a little juicy gossip here or there is common. Sound familiar? All clans, families, pods of people, have their black sheep. We have novelty, humor, and some rough-housing.

The South is certainly not a utopian society, because no one is perfect. A little ruckus here and there is good. It makes us normal. And let's admit it: all cultures have a little messin' around and no one can throw rocks at the other. Such 'going-ons' in Southern culture can be compared to soap operas. Ours could be called *The Edge of the Ferry* or *As the Ferry Turns*.

Everyone in the South knows that when you marry (or join/combine) into a family tree, you not only marry the trunk, but you also become a part of the whole tree. That includes the limbs, branches, leaves, and the critters that attach themselves to the tree.

In Galivants Ferry, no one asked me these particular questions 'cause they already knew about my people and me. Instead, they would get up close with squinty eyes and wrinkled forehead and ask rhetorically with tongue in cheek "You ain't one of them Hollidays are ya'?"

I never understood this question – how did they know who I was? I was a child and certainly didn't know exactly who they were but I knew we were all "family" in the country sides of Galivants Ferry. We were "kinfolks" 'cause we lived so close together geographically.

Sometimes this question hurt my feelings – what did they mean? My parents raised me right. We were no better than anyone else – so why did I hear a sarcastic tone in some of their remarks? Sure we had this big white house with columns, big magnolia trees to climb and a big red barn, country store and a fillin' station. They thought we were rich!

This is a still a mystery to me today, for one reason: to me, "rich" means a loving family, warm surroundings, security and friends, along with lots and lots of animals to hug.

Parents who lived through the Great Depression and World War II raised me. You didn't buy anything on credit. If you really needed it, you paid cash. Shopping for clothes was a twice a year event – a drive to Charleston, SC, for fall/winter school clothes and then another for spring/summer attire. This only occurred after you had tried on everything you owned to see what could be hemmed up, let out, or repaired. My grandmother, Mamanche – Blanche Russell, took care of all of this. After all, why spend money on a seamstress when you had one in the family? I went to public schools and was taught "everyone was born equal," so if I ever had a birthday party, or end of year swimming party the whole class would be invited. Back then, it was very rare to have a pool in your back yard.

I was a tomboy completely, climbing trees, riding ponies and donkeys, playing in the big red barn, dragging behind wagons and shooting BB guns. I was always covered in scabs, scars, bruises, and broken bones. If you didn't play outside you did not have anything to do. I remember looking at my scabby legs in puberty thinking – will I ever have pretty legs with no scabs or bruises? I still don't have them today and I am still a tomboy.

My best friend was my first cousin, Judson. We were neighbors and did everything together. We didn't have a choice and we would not have had it any other way. He was a year older. He taught me how to shoot guns, climb trees, build pine thicket huts, tree houses, and later on, other "things" (which I will tell you later). He was my hero. Living out in the country, with no phone long distance lines, no drivers' licenses – we were glued at the waist – and it was okay by me!

Now, before I go any further down my personal memories of the South I knew, it is important for you to know more about your family roots.

You three are a part of the fifth generation to live in Galivants Ferry. Your forefathers lived and died here, not a half-mile from our home place today. That is rare. How could five generations stay in the same home place – much less county, vicinity, or a small township? Let's look back into time to see how did we get here, why did we stay, how were we able to remain and prosper. To top it off, why in the world would anybody want to isolate themselves here?

You will find in these reminiscences not only your family history, but also much of the history of the South, and all of the reasons why this will forever be the home of my heart – the heart I give to you.

# PART I
## A Family Tree of Characters Grows

# The War of North Aggression

The War of the Northern Aggression...this is what Southerners call The Civil War.

I know you all have heard this expression, especially from your Granddaddy. It just came out of his mouth like it was the real name of the war. The same way your Uncle Joe used to call all tax people "The Russians." They had their own way of thinking about the past, and I think a lot of people still think the way they did. Daddy said he and his ancestors treated people nicely and fairly. They took care of each other.

For the most part, this war of the northern aggression did attack the Old South. Just like you saw it in *Gone with the Wind*. Y'all remember that classic movie. Those Yankees did come down and mess up the old South's life style. They were getting along just fine 'til Sherman started burning down entire cities and homes and telling Southerners who could work for whom and how they would get paid. The history of this time is so interesting. Ask your Daddy. He's so well read on this subject. I bet he knows more than most Civil War History teachers.

Even though Lincoln's troops did win and the way of life was drastically changed, the old south still lingers in Galivants Ferry and most of the "South." Now, there are always those bad apples that spoil the whole lot (your granddaddy would refer to this concept by saying "there is something rotten in Denmark"), but for the most part, the good that lingers is the silver lining, the cream of the crop, the light at the end of the tunnel.

Southerners (at least the ones in my mind) treat people with respect, regardless of color, race, religion, or nationality. Call me an optimist, but I choose to think this way. We all want to do what we can to make sure 'such and such' has what they need. It's called caring for your neighbor. Don't get me wrong; this doesn't refer only to Southerners. This is the way good people all over treat others, and we do not have a patent on this behavior. We just started it (so to speak).

It is simply having good manners, living your life according to the "Golden Rule" and being open minded best you can.

All three of you have lived in Charleston, where the first shot of the Civil War was fired. You have walked the Battery, visited Fort Sumter and Fort Moultrie. Imagine how the families' lives were changed forever. It still upsets me, even though I was not there. Just wish they had given us a choice about certain things.

And don't forget, you all had lots and lots of relatives go to The Citadel. A Citadel Cadet fired the first shot! They tried their best to maintain a certain way of life, but at least the good still remains. I am certain there were lots of bad things about life in the South that went away because of the war. I'm just glad we have gentle memories of this glorious era.

# The Holliday Family Tree

Your family tree has so many roots, branches, and limbs that it's hard to simplify it. And that's just the Holliday side. But I'm going to try.

If you all want to really investigate it there is plenty of material for you to sift through. It's all being saved for future generations and I have copied many documents for you written by previous generations.

Ok, here it is: There were three Holliday brothers that came to this country. One settled in Virginia. One of his descendants was at one time governor of that state. The second went to North Carolina, his name being Joseph William Holliday. The third brother went west. Of this branch we really do not have any record.

One Joseph William Holliday of the North Carolina branch married Tylitha Corburn, daughter of Jessie Corburn, one of Francis Marion's (The Swamp Fox) men of Revolutionary fame.

Joseph William Holliday and Tylitha Corburn had three sons and (I think) two daughters. Henry, or Harry as he is sometimes called, went to the State of Texas. He had two sons, Gus and Joseph, also two daughters, Mary and Mattie.

Joseph William II (February 14, 1827- April 30, 1904) came to South Carolina from Little Washington, North Carolina as a young man and settled in Horry County, moving where he could buy a good growth of pines for turpentine. It is said that he came to Horry County South Carolina in February 1852. He accumulated quite a bit of property during his lifetime. His parents died when he was quite young and the property that was left to be his brothers and sisters was taken by their guardians. He was what was termed a self-made man. He did not take up arms during the War Between the States, as the Governor wanted him to look after the women and children left behind and also to look after the Confederate salt works on the coast.

Because he was deprived of an education, he was determined that his children should have those opportunities that had been denied him. So each child was sent to some of the very best colleges of their day.

He did not care about nay show or splurge. He had a high regard for religion but never made any pretense at religion. He gave the land and material to build the little Galivants Ferry Baptist church. This church is used today for worship and stands as a memorial to him and his two companions. Mr. Holliday died at his home on Galivants Ferry Plantation on April 30, 1904. He is buried between his two wives at Rose Hill Cemetery in Marion, South Carolina.

Your South Carolina Holliday roots begin here.

Your Granddaddy, my father John Monroe Johnson Holliday, always liked to say he was born, lived, and would die in Galivants Ferry. He did. Perhaps this inherited gene is why we still call Galivants Ferry home.

From 1852 to 2012 is 160 years…WOW! I'd never done the math. That's a long time for on family to stay in one place!! I assume each generation passed down the love for the "home place." Let's see if we can keep it going.

Back to the family line. Your great, great grandfather, Joseph William Holliday II (1827-1904) married his first wife Miss Mary Elizabeth Grissette on December 19, 1859. They had about 8 children. I'll list them for you:

Jessie Gray (1860-1940), born September 26, 1860, married Miss Sallie Norman Davis of Marion South Carolina. They had three children who survived and three who died, including Christian, my namesake. He was in the livery stable business, J.W. Holliday and Son. After his first wife died he married Miss Bessie Godbolt of Marion South Carolina. They had four daughters (Bessie, Edna, Sara, and Via).

Capitola "Cap" was the first daughter, born December 26, 1861. She married James William ("Billie") King. They had Eugene, Ernest, Joseph Willis, Capitola (the oldest daughter), Mary and Mollie.

Mary Josephine ("Mollie") Married William Andrew Johnson. (1863) Annie Loula (1865-1939) married a Rev. John McMillan of North Carolina and they had nine children. One daughter was Louise, who is responsible for this family data. The other daughter was Montague, a distinguished professor at Limestone College for years who, like Louise, never married.

Joseph William III (Joe)(1867-1938) married Miss Lulie Mayo of Conway. He was a large planter in Williamsburg and Florence counties in South Carolina. They had six children. The details are sketchy. They had a Mary Elizabeth, a John Mayo who married Blanche Taylor, a Joseph William IV who married Leona Jones, a Paul, and a Henry who married a lady named Francis and a Robert E. ("Bob") who married Elizabeth Benson.

Claude Bernice (1868-1931) She married Samuel Davis from North Carolina. Henry, a son, who died after only a few days. Ruby Earnestine (1873-1954). She never married and lived with her sister Mollie.
George Judson (1875-1941). He is your great grandfather and served as a state senator in Horry County. He married your great grandmother Flora Johnson (1875-1929), on June 19, 1901. She was from Marion. Their offspring totaled nine children, which I want to list.

First they had twins George Judson II and a little brother who died in infancy (1902). George died at age three (1906). Floramay (1903) who married Dr. James C. McLeod of Florence. They had four children Flora Johnson, James C. II, George Holliday (1934-1960) and Florence Allen "Florie" (1940- )

Emma Johnson (1906-1962) married Harold Collins from Spartanburg. They had three children: Harold Jr. (1933), James McLeod (1937), and Emma (Emmaday) Holliday (1942). Reubie (1908- ) married David Gaston from Chester, SC. They had two children Virginia (1933) and Auther (1937).

Louise (1909- ) married John J. Deifell. They had Louise Holliday (Holly) (1936), John J. Jr. (1939) and Ann (Judson) (1945). Joseph William V (1912) married France Fields from Kingston NC. They had three children. J.W. Holliday (1942), Betty Tull (19450) and Judson Johnson (1952).

Martha Elizabeth (1914) married a first cousin of Dr. James C. McLeod. Dr. Edwin Allen II of Florence. They had three children: Elizabeth II (Betsy) (1938), Celeste (1942), and Edwin III (1945).

John Monroe Johnson (1916-2000), my daddy and your granddaddy, was named for his maternal grandfather, John Monroe Johnson. He married my Mama Marjorie Russell (b.1920) from Florence, SC. Their children are of course, me, Christian Monroe Holliday (b.1954), Marjorie Russell Holliday (b.1949) your aunt Russell) and my brother George Judson Holliday (1945-1967) your late Uncle George.

### 

    This may seem a little complicated, but now I want to take you back to your great, great grandfather. It just seems the easiest way to show you all how our family trees are so full of branches and leaves that have somewhat disappeared or we are not aware of.
    When Joseph William Holliday II lost his first wife, Mary Elizabeth Grissette to TB in 1889. He then married her youngest sister Miss Mildred (Nettie) Grissette in 1891. They had three children Winnifed (Winnie) who married John Cole of Conway, SC. Francis Grissette, a son, who married Anni Epps of Timmonsville, SC., and Nettie Maude who married Dr. W.C. Adams of Roland N.C.
    When your great, great, grandfather died he was buried between his two wives at Rose Hill in Marion, SC. It was a tradition of sorts. You have many, many relatives buried at this cemetery including my brother George and your granddaddy John Monroe.

This brings us to the fourth generation (21 first cousins). I am the youngest of the 21 cousins, so there is a huge age difference among us all. I have not charted these marriages yet, nor their children, which are also fifth generations along with you three. Most of my first cousins did marry and had children that have given birth to the sixth generation! As you can see we are behind nearly two whole generations! I've been talking to others in the family and we are just realizing there is a generation of grown adults who do not know each other! And now with some seventh generations arriving, we are really behind!

Let's work together to put all the puzzles together. We owe it to our ancestors to keep the tree growing. Keeping up with the ones in Galivants Ferry is easy but the rest of the leaves of this tree will require help form some cousins I have in mind!

# Aunt Floramay

God broke the mold when Aunt Floramay was born.

She was truly one of a kind…the true Southern Belle. She was the eldest of nine children born to your great grandmama and great granddaddy. Mr. and Mrs. George Judson Holliday. She was the first-born daughter and your granddaddy was the baby. She was the very first Miss South Carolina, which they called Miss Palma Festa after the state tree, the Palmetto. Y'all's Great Aunt Floramay had personality plus.

I remember her telling how people from all over would come to visit her at the Ferry. There were sleeping porches for the guests as it took time for visitors to get there and you didn't want to rush them off. She always told me, "Boys come to see you, Christy, even if it's a long drive. You never go see them." I also remember her telling my sister Russell, "Go on to the party. If they had known you were in town they would have invited you. Just go in and act like you are supposed to be there."

She was always dressed to the nines. Her hair was long and she swept it up in a coiffure held with beautiful hairpins. She wore the most magnificent diamond broach I have ever seen every moment of every day. It fit her. She even wore it on her blue nightgowns and her navy blue bathing suit.

Your great granddaddy George bought several thousand acres in 1924 at a beach in South Carolina. He named it Floral Beach after his wife Flora and their daughter Floramay. They built a large sprawling beach cottage known as "Happy Hollidays." I was told they spent their summers there with lots of family and friends. I think your grandfather was about 8-years-old then.

I will never forget Floramay's funeral. She was such a jovial person she would not have wanted people to be unhappy and she loved to be in the middle of the party. It was an open casket in the living room of her beautiful antebellum home. People chatted, telling stories and reminiscing about her. She looked beautiful as always. Cocktails were placed on the edges of her casket. She was there enjoying every minute of it or at least that's what I remember thinking.

What a gal. One of a kind.

# True Southern Belles

All Southern Belles know what is and is not proper. Whether they follow the rules of being belles is up to them.

When I was growing up, my father's sisters were the epitome of this female genre. All five of were so graceful, self-assured, polite and "dressed to the nines" all the time. They took care of their man, their table manners were impeccable, and of course, they wore appropriate jewelry for the occasion. Church was a given. Another Southern Belle tradition was using Tiffany's wedding invitations and stationary. These were watermarked and engraved and were part of special occasions.

Unfortunately, most of the occasions in which we were able to mingle took place only during funerals and weddings. I've already told you about Aunt Floramay, the very first Miss South Carolina. The others were equally as personable in their own special ways. Each had distinctive manners befitting a classic Southern Belle. They had been raised properly and knew their Emily Post manners backwards and forwards. They treated me like I was special. Being the youngest child of their baby brother made me truly the youngest niece, so being "babied" was fun and I could tell their interests were genuine.

My Aunt Elizabeth lived in Florence, South Carolina in a big old antebellum home on Cherokee Road. She had lots of weddings in her yard and I remember the candles lit under domes. The sweet smells of magnolias and honeysuckle, coupled with the ambience created by the manicured southern yard, made for delightful afternoon and evening soirees.

Aunt Floramay lived right down the street from Aunt Elizabeth. That was nice; an afternoon of visiting them with my father was a special and rare time. Both houses had beautiful gardens and nice gentlemen in white coats that took care of the yard and home. The old cobble stone brick walkways, camellias, large linked magnolias and the huge matured azaleas had been there for years. Walking through the grounds made you feel like you were walking in a storybook where huge swings, fountains with gold fish, horses in stable and outdoor rooms separated by hedges and gardens created a maze of southern nostalgia.

The inside of both their homes were indicative of Southern Belles as well. You had hardwood floors, large living rooms and formal dining rooms with shiny old silver, chandeliers, oriental rugs and wooden staircases leading to at least three floors with lots of nooks and crannies, warm dens with real fireplaces, sitting rooms and a huge family kitchen with butler pantries. Plus, they had help that were always treated and loved just like blood kin. They wore white crisp uniforms and acted like they knew you, even if they didn't.

Visiting these old Southern homes and exploring the antique covered rooms filled with thousands of family photographs, formal portraits and of course the family guest book made for rich, meaningful interludes. We were always welcomed, even if we appeared unannounced. I loved it and received special treatment by my Southern Belle Aunts.

My three aunts – Ruby, Louise, and Emma – lived further away. I did not get to visit with them in their homes, but when we were together, they made me feel just as loved as their other nieces and nephews. They were all very striking and very independent. All Southern Belles are distinctive; they were equally unique. I remember they wore pearls, hats, white gloves at times, and wardrobes of fine suits, distinctive frocks with matching pocketbooks and pump high heels.

I also remember they hugged a lot. When you saw them, they would say, "I'm your aunt such and such," and they'd tell me stories about Daddy and living at the Ferry. They would each tell me who they married, who their children were and make it a point to introduce me to them. That might sound strange to y'all – not knowing all your first cousins – but as the youngest, there was a big age difference between a lot of the first cousins and me. You see, nothing is more important to Southern Belles than family. Family is your heritage. Family is so critical to Southerners. You just have to know your kin! My Daddy made sure I went to every wedding and funeral; otherwise, we would not know where we came from!

I think there was a schism in your granddaddy's family. I don't know the details, since I wasn't there, but it created a rift between Daddy, his brother Joe and his sisters. Your grandmamma and granddaddy had to elope during this period of time. Mamanche, your grandmother's mother, took Mama to the train station in Florence, and sent her on to Charleston to marry your granddaddy. I'm glad I wasn't there. I will say, it appeared during my childhood that this rift was righted 'cause everyone got along fine.

Why am I telling y'all this? It's because I don't want y'all to ever have a rift between the three of you. It's against the rules, and since I am now almost a Southern Belle, whatever I say is good for y'all. So there! In addition, keeping up with your cousins and family tree folks is very important otherwise you might drift away from your roots. That is a big no-no in the South. Remember: Blood is thicker than water. When necessary, to end a squabble, sometimes the "mountain has to go to Mohammed" (Aunt Elizabeth used to say this). It's okay to say you're sorry, even if you're not.

# Po' Southern Belles:
## Ain't No Help Rounds These Parts No' Mo'

Keeping my mouth shut is a problem for me.

Sometimes, blurting out or standing firm on a subject I am not normally involved with can be good or bad. Although it's rare that I keep my mouth shut; if I pray this small prayer prior to certain occasions I attend, like a meeting or event, a miracle can take place. God gives me (and you, too, if you ask) words, no words, actions, or no actions. For someone like me who loves to talk, it takes discipline to keep quiet or say very little or just listen while I bite my tongue. The small prayer above plus this family one my father always opened meetings with really help. Here is the one my poppa said before any decisions were made at our small office in Galivants Ferry:

"God, let us make the right decisions for the right reasons."
True Southern Belles were blessed mightily. They had people like Jenny Lou. There were others who helped us but Jenny Lou was a true classic. (Y'all soon read my story about her 'cause she was the epitome of "The Help" in the 1950s and 1960s.)

Jenny Lou wore crisp white uniforms with matching hat piece. They lived with us like family and put us in their family bibles. They made sure we ate well, had clean underwear (just in case we got in a wreck), inserted Biblical phrases in normal conversation and made sure we had good manners. She would say statements like, "You best straighten up! You knows better than dat. I raised you better. Them others just won't raised right."

Then she'd look at me, try to hide her smile but the twinkle in her eye showed how much she loved me. She just wanted to make sure her 'girl' (me) knew right from wrong and that I stayed on God's side of life. She made sure her "chillins" (me, my sister Russell and my brother George) didn't stray too far out of the Southern "box."

Jenny Lou is in heaven now. I miss her. Not just cause she took care of me, fed me, washed and ironed my clothes, and was the best chaperone in the world…No, not just those things. She was family and she was my other mother. I know I will see her again one day. I still love her.

"God, please serve Jenny Lou like she's ordering room service. I bet she never had room service before. Please, one time? Also, if possible, could someone else wash her clothes and starch and iron them just right? Thank you, God."

Oh my, where was I going with this story? Sometimes my mind jumps around but everything I have written so far is very important. Oh Yeah! I wanted to tell y'all that the life of a Southern Belle has changed dramatically. You all have seen the decline in your short lives. Okay, when I grew up in Galivants Ferry, we had Jenny Lou, and Jenny Lou even had a helper most of the time. We had William, Willie, LB, Billy, JW, JW's family (especially his daddy who drove my daddy around), Aaron, Clyde, and many others…All these folks were our extended family. Of course Grand Mama ran a tight ship at home but we couldn't have done it all without help.

Guess what, y'all? Ain't no' help no' mo' in these here parts. That's why I feel the word "po'" (short for poor…not in a money sense but in loss of way of life) should be a prefix for Southern Belle, at least not like I grew up with. My cousin Florrie feels the same way. She is the daughter of Aunt Floramay, and she tells me every time she sees me that she is the "help" now – not the white coated men to which I referred in the Floramay story. Beats me why I built such a big house. I reckon I thought things would be the same but times have changed for sure. What in the world was I thinking! I have gotten some help since I wrote this but ain't no telling how long it will last.

Don't get me wrong…We are blessed beyond our wildest dreams. I think you would call me a transitional Southern Belle/Po Belle. The recession (also known as the little depression after 9/11) has taken a toll, but we Southerners are very resistant to much change and we are strong. It's hard to do what it takes to hang on to being a Southern Country Lady. It sho' was easier when Daddy was here, but he is gone, too, so I'm just gonna keep learning to do things I thought I couldn't do and growing spiritually and pray that my help stays. "Dear God, please help me hang on to my help."

Moving to the Ferry has not been easy for any of us, but I am still glad we made the move. Hope you are glad in some way, also. Anyway, I can attest that after being here for 12 years it did not take long to discover things ain't what they used to be. Life is wonderful; it's just different. Stumbling blocks become steppingstones. I do count my blessings.

We still got big homes, the kind with columns and spiral staircases, formal living room that no one goes into, and butler pantries (A butler? What is that?). The grape vines still produce, the vegetable garden is gone since the guineas and peacocks eat the seeds, but you can find fresh vegetables elsewhere. The fig trees are abundant, the fishing and hunting are still great, the farmers farm a variety of crops (not just tobacco), and we still love our community where we all feel related. Society ways of the Old South still exist, too. You know, the debutante balls with long white gloves, full-length dresses and tails for the men. I do not think any of that will change but no one is helping you get dressed like in Gone with the Wind. It's fun to dress up and play make-believe.

People still call me Miss Christy and your daddy, Mr. David. We do hold tight to our Southern traditions….real tight. But we do share. People do care about their neighbors and I hope no one is hungry. We try to help each other if we are aware of their plights. It's part of being a Southerner. We share our hunting land, too, with many and love having soirees. We cling to old ways with tight-fisted grips. We have been accused of hanging on to land we can't afford. A true Southerner will cling on to the past and traditions 'til it hurts. I say again that we do share as best we can. I hope others think that about us but I might as well worry about a hurricane as to worry what others think about us. People got to have something to gossip about. Others can't understand this unless you live through a life of whispers or know a Po Southern Belle personally. Ask Jane Graves. She knows. She knows me 'bout as well as anyone cause we grew up together.

Okay, my precious children, I have gone through this recollection to tell you some things you might not be aware of, but the real reason is I do not want any of you to be stuck in a past that you were not a part of. You can, if you want to, but the decision is up to y'all. Sometimes you have to make a clean break and embark on a new life. You all can do anything you set your mind to. You can go live anywhere and if you change your mind you can always come back to the Ferry. Might not have any help, so just know that! Do not bring me dirty clothes to wash. Now, grandbabies are a different story.

I love help. I want some help. If I can't have good help this book will never be finished. Help has been underrated for years. I reckon we took it for granted but I do not now take anything for granted. We all need help, not only to help with chores but to be our friends, be honest with us, put us in our place and share their lives with us. Help is extended family. When you follow the Golden Rule, things are just better all the way around. "Do unto others as you would have them do unto you." I don't think y'all will ever forget that. Everyone needs others. In conclusion I would like to say a little prayer.

"God, please help me have help. They are family to me, and part of my spiritual family, too. God, Bless them all…and me, too. I like to think that I am help to my help, like blood sisters and a prayer partner."

# Southern Gentlemen

Men can be Southern Belles in their own masculine way. We call them Southern Gentlemen.

Even way back when, they were few and far between. There just weren't ever a lot of them anywhere! Why? Well, lots of men can look and act up front like a Southern Gentleman, but it's the things they didn't do and didn't say that made them true Southern Gentlemen.

The most outstanding of these rare gems is alive today. His name is James C. McLeod. He's your second cousin on your granddaddy's side of the family. Your Great Aunt Floramay (the first Palma Festa, Miss South Carolina) was his Mama and his daddy was Dr. James C. McLeod Sr., founder of the McLeod Hospital in Florence. He was born and raised in Florence, SC. Holly, he presented you at the Tarantella debutante ball. Those long white gloves events were so much fun dancing with Southern Gentleman. They made us feel like princesses for the night.

James (Jimmy) is a soft-spoken, elegant man. He's tall with dark hair, perfectly built and his words flow from his mouth like sweet honey. To my knowledge, not an unkind gesture has ever left his lips. You can't come into a room without him standing up or pulling your chair back or opening a door. I remember the time when we couldn't get Jimmy in his car because he had to open all the doors for the women. He just would not get in first! I'm not sure how we managed to get him in the car!

His eyes speak the truth with an aura of kindness. His dimples are permanent from always wearing a smile. That doesn't mean Southern Gentlemen can't cry or show sadness. They just know when and how to express their feelings.

In an addition to having exceptional southern manners, Jimmy is also a wonderful husband and daddy. I'm sure his father and mother taught him these "almost extinct" qualities. They were taught to them by their families and passed down from previous generations.

Wonder if it's too late to pass them down to future generations? I think we can, but it'll take a lot of work.

# The Other Hollidays

This may seem strange to y'all, but we truly referred to each other's families as "the other Hollidays."

There were many other Holliday relatives, but the two sons of George and Flora were the ones who carried on the Holliday name in Galivants Ferry. Anyway, to me, the "Other Holliday's" are the Joseph W. Holliday family.

My Uncle Joseph married Francis Fields from Kinston, NC. She and Joseph had three children, Billy, Betty, and Judson who are my first cousins. We were kissing cousins, so to speak. We all went to the same church and shared all that Galivants Ferry had to offer. We were very close. We still are. Only my brother George is missing. If something happens to one of us, I'm sure the others will come to the rescue. It's like friends who don't see each other for a long time, but when you see them, it's like no time has passed and you've never been apart. I've never thanked them for the support they gave the entire family when George died.

Aunt Francis was always an eccentric, attractive woman. She was intelligent, well read, an avid bridge player and an accomplished gardener. Her yard was always filled with something blooming, along with lots of pedigree Boxer dogs. She never did anything halfway. Frances was and still is a yellow-dawg Democrat. She loved the Kennedys, the Beatles, and most of all Elvis Presley. (Don't even try to take one of Elvis' scarves from her). In her younger years, she taught Sunday school and was a competitive bridge player. Francis was the very first health nut I ever knew. She knew about organic ways before we ever heard of them!! Brewers Yeast was a household item in her kitchen, along with sliced bologna and homemade Brunswick stew. She was passionate at whatever interested her at the time.

The best time I personally had with Frances was on a trip to Egypt and Morocco. Your daddy and I went there on a Citadel trip for our honeymoon. Frances, Judson's wife Cheryl, plus Frances' two friends, Grace Smith and Harriett Buchan, were also passengers on this incredible trip. Traveling down the Nile with Frances was a blast. We hired Josef, an Egyptian buggy driver, in Luxor for an evening. We were riding down streets looking for a store that sold Scotch Liquor. It was 'nervy' exciting.

The flight to Abu Simbel was an adventure as well. The whole trip down the Nile and onto Morocco was just as amazing. Visiting Marrakech, Rabat and Fez, was like being in *Casablanca* with Humphrey Bogart and Ingrid Bergman. We visited ancient tombs, watched snakes slither out of baskets, and were entertained by belly dancers, to name a few exotic experiences. Frances was very wary of any of the foreigner merchants. I don't think she ever exchanged money because she did not want to be "hoodooed." She, Grace and Harriett were all a riot. They were a fun trio to hang out with.

Uncle Joe, my father's older brother, was a good-looking, charismatic man. He had the thickest hair – just gorgeous. Marvin Skipper told me he was a "shrewd businessman." He was in charge of the farming end of the business and was solely in charge of the business in Galivants Ferry while Daddy was in WWII. He loved going to the tobacco market in Fairmont.

Joe graduated from the Citadel. He played golf well, competed in tennis tournaments throughout the state, and loved hunting. He was a well-rounded, well-liked man. I was proud to call him my uncle. After my brother George died, I feel Joe was especially attentive to me. I remember him playing with me in the snow and taking me to a duck farm. We got along great 'til I moved back to Galivants Ferry after my first marriage. I started working in the family business and I tried to bring the city to the country. I knew just enough to be dangerous. I really think Joseph listened more than daddy. Neither wanted any changes at all. They had gotten along just swell for 100 years, so why change now? Now as I get older, I like the old ways better, too.

Joe was a healthy individual, also. I think he was the very first committed 'walker' I ever knew. Every morning like clockwork, he walked from his house to the Galivants Ferry Church and back. That was a two-mile walk, which was not common at the time. His son Billy used to remind him, "Daddy if you don't wind the clock up, it'll run down." This metaphor kept him walking! Unfortunately, Uncle Joe died of a heart attack. He told his family to stay together and they have. He was buried at Rose Hill Cemetery in Marion, South Carolina. Rose Hill is packed with lots of y'alls relatives.

Uncle Joseph and Aunt Frances' first born, Billy, is a Holliday through and through. Thick light brown hair, blue eyes, tall and smart. He was one of the last eligible bachelors in these parts 'til his wife Harriett snagged him. She got a good one – and vice versa. Billy is talented. He plays the piano and harmonica by ear, and his boogie–woogie will bring down the house. He's a great shag dancer, too. He loves beach music. I remember one evening he came to visit me in my room to practice a new dance step. Even though we were not the same age, he and I hung out. Those times made me feel special.

Billy went to Aynor Elementary School, Asheville School for boys, and graduated from Washington and Lee University. He is a wonderful writer and has been published in various publications. He actually has compiled an oral history of Horry County at Coastal Carolina University where you can hear some of the old timers reciting the history of the area. Billy is responsible for getting me interested in the history around here. He is much more precise than me because he works from facts and I work from recollections. To each his own, I reckon. One of his larger "piece de la resistance" was his in-depth study of and writing about Doc Holliday. Unfortunately, it was before computers, and when his house burned down, so did the manuscript.

In the summer of 2011, I visited the resting place of Doc Holliday in Colorado. I brought him back a surprise from there, a photograph of Doc's tombstone.

Billy is also a staunch Democrat. He is the spokesperson for the Galivants Ferry Stump, along with my sister Russell. He opens up the Stump and puts on one hell of a super halftime show with his harmonica playing Cannon Ball Express.

Betty Tull Holliday is just as interesting, and has diverse talents and passions like the rest of her family. She, too, was one of the first really healthy people I ever knew. I guess it just ran in the family. Even though they had Tina Wiggins as a country cook, they knew how to make meals healthy, too. Betty also went to Aynor Schools, then off to Salem boarding school in North Carolina before graduating from Converse College in Spartanburg, South Carolina. She was very close to my brother George, as was Billy.

Betty married David McLeod from Florence, SC. They have one child, Frances Fields McLeod. Betty is another trooper. She has been through some life trials and stays positive. She is a role model for me. She is also the very first Vegan I've ever known! When all of us were eating white rice, white bread and white potatoes, Betty knew what to eat instead. She was a pioneer, in my mind.

Betty Tull, as she likes to be called, plays tennis, jogs, goes on meditation retreats (also a pioneer in this area), cooks, gardens and takes care of her family. That is a lot. I hear she's also a great Mah-Jong Player. Betty is an integral part of the Galivants Ferry Stump, too. Need I say she's a 'died in the wool' Democrat as well! And of course, she loves Elvis and the Kennedys. We Hollidays are kinda set in our ways. In my opinion, that's a good thing!

I forgot one thing: Betty is the only woman I know who has never dyed or had a permanent put in her hair. She is 'all natural', and she looks many years younger than she is. Good genes.

Joseph and Frances' baby is Judson. I've written a whole separate story about him because we were 'attached at the waist' growing up. His story comes next!

All in all, I love "the other Hollidays." We children were like "six peas in a pod." When you were raised in a place like Galivants Ferry, you were all part of the same patch of peas, and your roots were firmly planted.

# Judson Holliday:
# My Best Friend, First Cousin, & Next Door Neighbor

Growing up in Galivants Ferry had its pros and cons. At the time, I did not know any cons existed. It was the only lifestyle I knew.

Y'all have seen the big difference first-hand between city life and country life. When your Daddy and I moved y'all from the big city of Greenville, South Carolina to itty bitty Galivants Ferry right smack dab in the middle of your puberty and adolescent years, y'all had a fit. I don't have to tell you it was a major culture shock. Y'all questioned our judgment. Holly, you even told me I had not thought this move through.

I give all the credit and blame to your Daddy. It was his idea, whether you believe me or not. He even reserved you all spots at Pee Dee Academy.

Sorry, I got off track. This is about my childhood, not y'alls.

If it hadn't been for Judson, my neighbor and first cousin, I don't believe it would be possible to conjure up so many happy early childhood memories. We were almost the same age and just a year apart in school. We had a whole lot in common.

One of my first memories of our time together was Judson coming over to my house on Christmas Eves. No tellin' how young we were. I vividly envision us running back and forth throughout the house, jumping on couches, peering through venetian blind windows, looking for Santa Claus and his reindeer. Our families fit together nicely. There were three children in Judson's family and three children in my family. Judson's older brother Billy and my brother George were close pals. Betty, Judson's sister, was about Russell's age so they hung out, and of course, Judson and I were thick as thieves.

Daddy's brother Joseph and his wife Frances would come over with the kids and visit my Mama and Daddy, eat a light supper and get ready for Santa with us. They were evenings of love, family fellowship, good food and fireworks which have left me with colorful sparkly memories…the kind that make you smile and make you wish you were a child again.

After school, Judson and I played together on most afternoons. We loved playing outside. When you grew up in the country, you learned how to entertain yourselves. If you ran out of stuff to do, you made things up. Going to a mall or a movie or visiting folks down the street wasn't an option. We did play occasionally with other kids in Galivants Ferry, but for the most part it was just the two of us.

We both had ponies, which we rode together on the pony road and sometimes to the "bone yard." The bone yard was a cool, spooky place where the dead animals were taken to rot. The pony road was and still connects Judson's old home and ours. It's a dirt road way off Highway 501, a busy dangerous highway, and the road to Myrtle Beach for tourists year-round. It was the only way for us to get together because we did not drive and we knew better than to mess with the heavy traffic on 501. The pony road was a safe, meandering dirt pathway, right next to a swampy area and bordered by fields and grape vines.

We would pretend we were near a jungle with wild animals that were going to jump out at you at any time. There might have been some wild animals there, but all I remember seeing was an occasional snake and running into huge spider webs with humongous hairy spiders. Maybe that's why I am deathly scared of spiders today. Some days Judson would ask Beelie, an employee of their family, to hitch up a green small wagon pulled by his pony. While Beelie drove the wagon, Judson and I would hold on to the rear for our lives as our bodies dragged through the dirt and mud puddles, seeing who could stay on the longest. What a blast! We got so dirty, the dirtier, the more fun.

We would end up at his house. Tina, their maid, would make us fried bologna sandwiches with the thick-sliced, country bologna. Boy, were they good.

We had lots of "favorite" activities, but one of our most memorable was climbing trees. Not just any old tree would do. Three ancient, huge Magnolia trees stood in my front yard. They all had huge trunks and fat limbs, with baby trees sprouting all around. Their canopies were so large that even if it was raining we could stay dry. We built tree houses in all of them. All the cousins contributed to the tree houses, but Judson and I considered them ours. Friends would come over to play, too, but for the most part just Judson and I played there by ourselves, adding onto them with hammers, nails, 1 x 8 beams, and any scrap lumber we could find.

One of the tree houses we had was three stories high. You had to climb up the steps we made by hammering in the scraps of wood on the huge trunk. The steps were dangerous and only the bravest would attempt to get to the top. We both were brave, so we used this area like the lookout of a pirate ship. Some days, we climbed up separate trees and pretended to shoot each other like cowboys and Indians. We pretended our apple juice was a saloon drink, and we'd carry our peanut butter sandwiches with us so we wouldn't have to get down from our hiding places if we got hungry. No one with any sense would come between our two tree houses nor sneak underneath them, for fear of an ambush.

Hunting was another favorite. Judson taught me how to shoot my BB gun with accuracy. I will never forget killing my first bird, a red bird, and excitedly running to show it to my mother who was having bridge club in our living room. I thought they would all be impressed. I was wrong. When I showed up, dirty and holding the dead bird, they thought it was horrible. Talk about bursting my bubble!

I learned from then on not to show anyone or tell any grown-ups about our hunting trips in the yard.

We also had lots of fun building straw forts in the thicket between our houses. Even the chiggers, no see-ums, and mosquitoes didn't keep us from this activity! It was the most fun when the new straw had just fallen. The straw had a wonderful pine scent and there was lots of it in which to jump. We built these lean-to's right behind Beelie and Martha Perritt's house. We liked to spy on them. They never knew it was us, but when they heard us, Martha would holler and shoot her .12-gauge single-barrel gun in the air to scare us off. It worked and we would run for our lives! It didn't take us long to come back. It was fun being scared.

In the summertime, the available activities changed. Both our families moved to the beach about 45 minutes away. Our houses were right down the street from each other so we could visit easily by strolling down the beach. Every morning, one of us would end up at the other's house in time to watch *The Three Stooges*. We learned how to do other things, like riding through campgrounds looking for girlfriends for Judson, going to every movie that came on, playing golf, surfing, fishing, crabbing, and eventually going to the night spots like The Beach Club. This spot was famous for groups like The Tams, The Drifters, Swinging Medallions, Platters, Marvin Lance, and Otis Redding, to name a few. We went as often as we could.

We loved the 60s. In addition to beach music and shagging, we loved the new music: Iron Butterfly. The Beatles. Elvis. You name it, we liked it. We were all about diversification when it came to music. It was the time of adolescence…growing up, feeling our oats and having parties at the pool in Galivants Ferry and at Judson's playroom across the street.

We both attended boarding schools for high school. I was a student at Ashley Hall while Judson went to Porter Gaud, both in Charleston. Back then, the boarding schools were very strict and you did not get out too often except for church on Sundays and an occasional Saturday afternoon. Dating was the privilege of a few – if you had good grades and you weren't on restriction.

Still, Judson and I were able to see each other every once in a while. He did not like being away from Galivants Ferry so somehow he got to go home. Little did he know he would then be sent to Asheville School for Boys in the western North Carolina Mountains, a good six hours away? He didn't like that, either. Aaron Peavy told me he would take Judson to school, drop him off, and Judson would beat him back home – by hitchhiking, he assumed. Judson finally prevailed, graduating from Aynor High School, the closest school to the Ferry.

Even when we weren't in the same area, we stayed in touch. We still had the summers at Myrtle Beach. Judson taught me how to smoke my first cigarette and drink my first beer... and he told me all about sex. This is what he said: In order to have sex, you needed a man and a woman, two twin beds, and a hose. The man got on one bed, the woman got on the other, and somehow a hose connected them. I believed him. He had never lied to me before, and he told me not to tell anyone.

This is the first time I have told this secret.

The college years found us back in the same city, Spartanburg, South Carolina (Sparkle City). He went to Wofford and I went to Converse. His was an all-boy school and mine was an all-girl school. It was predestined that we stayed close. After all, we were best friends and family and everybody needs your best buddy nearby.

Eventually, Judson married Cheryl Crumpler. They have two super kids, Joseph and Johnson, and y'all know they are our neighbors back in Galivants Ferry. The world seems to go around in circles. We might not see each other like we used to, since raising you youngins is a full-time job, but we know that if we ever need each other, all one of us has to do is holler.

# Daddy Russell

Your great grandfather on the Russell side of the family was a jeweler and an optician. What a combination of professions!

I know he robbed the cradle and married Blanche Register, my grandmama. We called her Mamanche. He and Mamanche, your great grandparents, were a happy couple. They were like two peas in a pod and raised four children. They were both very hard workers.

Daddy Russell loved to fish. He was the best fresh water angler around these parts. Santee was his stomping ground. He and Mamanche had a house on the river where we'd all go visit in the summertime. On this huge fresh water lake in South Carolina, I learned how to improve my fishing skills by using special Southern bait. The Catawba worms grow on a Catawba tree. All you had to do was pluck the squiggle green worm off the tree, put it on your hook and you were guaranteed a mighty fine fish for supper. Many first cousins learned how to water-ski here. We had a blast.

I'm going to tell y'all something I've never told you before. If it had not been for Daddy Russell, we would not have access Mary Long Lakes. It was his idea to build up the roads that lead to these three oxbow lakes. You've seen them. These three lakes lay adjacent to the Little Pee Dee River. Somehow he talked my daddy and Uncle Joseph into spending money to build these roads. It could not be done today due to wetland laws. This piece of property is a gem in the rough thanks to your great granddaddy and his love for fishing. "Sho' nuff!"

I'll never forget catching the train from Florence, South Carolina to Florida. It was my first train ride, first time visiting another state and first time I saw an orange tree. It was a special trip because it was finally my turn to go with my grandparents to Florida to visit his family.

Daddy Russell and Mamanche also loved chickens and chicken yards. They had a miniature farm in the middle of Florence. You got to have chickens in order get the fresh eggs. Plus, how else can you get rid of the leftover food scraps? Chickens are like disposals. Gama did it, I do it, and I bet y'all will do it, too.

Towards the end of Daddy Russell's life he was in the hospital dying from emphysema. His family was gathered to say goodbye to him. All of a sudden, he opened his eyes and looked at my Mama, your grandma. He told her to tell George, her son, to bring his golf clubs to heaven. Reassuringly he told mama, George would like it there.

Five years later your Uncle George died. How did Daddy Russell foretell this tragic death? We know where Daddy Russell and George are now.

# Mamanche

I wish y'all could have known your maternal great-grandmother Mamanche.

Her real name was Blanche, but her first granddaughter, Margy, could not say Blanche so they called her Ma Manche — short for Mama Blanche. She was the only person in my family that approved of my first marriage to Perrin Trotter. I was 19 when we got engaged and 20 when we married. Mamanche's husband 'Daddy Russell' married Mamanche at 16 years of age. He robbed the cradle and got himself a gem. Mamanche thought 20 was plenty old to get married. I will never forget how supportive she was, even though the marriage did not work out. We were just too young.

Mamanche and Daddy Russell had four children: Sam, Ethel, Pug, and your grandma Margy. They also raised Louise Lambright. She was another sister to them and another aunt to me. Back then; people took care of their people. What has happened to that practice today? Uh, oh, I'm going off on a tangent…got to stick with the subject. But I really wish we still treated each other with that kind of respect today.

The best memories I have of Mamanche are the times we cooked together with Reubie. Reubie was like Jenny Lou, who raised me. Reubie had a beautiful smile. Her lips really looked like rubies and her long bronzed arms and legs permeated Mamanche's kitchen. She was a southern lady and the best fried chicken cook in the world. Her biscuits were locally famous, too. She definitely knew her way around a Southern kitchen! If I had not spent all those times with Mamanche and Reubie, I do not think I would be able to cook, much less want to cook.

Mamanche taught me how to cook her famous vegetable soup. Here's the recipe.

## Mamanche's Vegetable Soup:
- 2 to 3 pounds of lean stew beef, cut into bite-sized pieces
- 2 to 3 large purple onions, diced up
- 16 ounces of canned chopped tomatoes (fresh if you have them)
- 1 large bag of frozen sliced okra
- 1 to 2 cups of chopped celery
- 1 large can of shoe peg corn (teeny corn)
- 1 large can of midget butter beans
- Lots and lots of shredded cabbage
- Bouillon cubes if you need them for extra taste
- Salt and pepper
- Tomatoes…if you have fresh cut them up and add to the mix…fresh never hurts

Put at least 4 quarts of water into a large boiler along with onions, tomatoes and beef. Bring to a boil and cook until the beef is tender. Add all other ingredients and cook slowly.

*Slowly stir so the ingredients won't stick to the bottom of the pot. There is nothing worse than cutting up and taking the time to get all the goodies in the pot, and then burning it. I have done it and it's just not the same; a little burnt flavor does not enhance the recipe.*

*Do not over-salt or pepper, since that hides the vegetables' flavor. Later, everyone can add whatever they like. The longer it cooks, the better it tastes…and even let sit overnight, put a lid on it and eat the next day. Delicious!*

### ###

I promise you this is the best vegetable soup in the world. The secret is the shredded cabbage. You cannot see it, but it provides bulk and a distinct taste. Do not tell anyone the secret. In a little while, I might even give you the secret biscuit recipe — and the secret pound cake recipe. From memory.

Besides memories in the kitchen, spending Christmas dinners and afternoons with Mamanche and Daddy Russell was a tradition. We would drive about an hour to Florence, South Carolina after Christmas morning at home in Galivants Ferry. Lots of our cousins from the Russell side of the family would come from all over. It was always a special day. We were allowed to bring one toy that Santa had given us so we could share with everyone. Of course, they shared with us too.

The dinner was always huge and scrumptious. Our "eyes were always bigger than our stomachs!" Mamanche's Christmas day menu was typically southern: turkey, fried chicken, ham, fresh vegetables (never canned), homemade dressing, biscuits that melted in your mouth, and her famous Pound Cake.

We all helped and even Reubie joined us for dinner. Back then, our help worked on holidays, but I think Reubie liked and wanted to be with us. She was family and all these cousins, aunts and uncles were her kin, too, plus they were from all over and it was rare to have everyone together. She wore an extra crisp white uniform with a new apron on Christmas. Her lips were red as roses and her white teeth so bright with her huge smile as she greeted us one at a time. Her long arms were extra good for hugs.

At the end of the day, my brother George, sister Russell and I would curl up in the back seat of daddy's big long Cadillac and fall asleep. Mama would wake us up singing, "Home again, home again, jiggety jog…" as we drove in the driveway in Galivants Ferry. Sweet dreams.

Oh yeah ... I got lost in the Mama side of Mamanche, but I need to tell you she was also ahead of her times as far as women's rights were concerned. She was the first modern woman I ever met. She worked not only at home, in her yard as a master gardener and kept up with her chicken yard in the middle of Florence, but she also managed her family farms in the Florence area. After Daddy Russell died, she took control of all details of the family farming business.

One day, she went to check on a farm and did not stop close enough to the stop sign before looking both ways and darted out into the path of another vehicle. She died on that tragic day.

Mamanche always told me I needed to make my own decisions, good or bad. She showed her support of new ideas, and for certain people, that was not always popular. She was a strong individual who led the way for us. She showed me I should never be afraid to step up, take action and stand up for what I believe. She knew a person would not always be right, but one needs to have the opportunity to try. You never know what you can do 'til you try.

Because of Mamanche, I am a stronger woman and I hope you all will be stronger people by following her example of pushing outside the box of expectations.

Oh, I almost forgot. Here is the recipe for Mamanche's Pound Cake.

## Mamanche's Pound Cake:

- *3 cups sugar*
- *2 sticks butter (room temperature)*
- *5 large brown eggs (fresh if you got 'em - room temperature)*
- *3 cups plain flour*
- *½ pint whipping cream*
- *1 tsp. vanilla*
- *1 tsp. lemon extract*

*Cream the sugar and butter together by hand, and then use a mixmaster. Add one egg at a time, whirring it the whole time. Beat each egg for at least a minute. Alternately add the flour and whipping cream, still whirring the whole time. Add the vanilla and lemon extract, and mix really well.*

*Next, pour the batter in a well-greased tube pan. Let the batter settle and lift an inch from the counter and drop it a few times. Just do it. You will see air bubbles come up. (I don't know why you do this, but you do. A lot of this recipe is superstitious and a bit spooky, but I promise you it will not come out well if you don't lift that batter off the counter.)*

*Put in a cold oven and then bake at 325 on the middle rack for at least one hour. Do not open the oven door. Turn on the oven light to peak and see if it's done. Get a broom (preferably clean), pluck one of its bristles out and stick in the cake after one hour. If the bristle is covered with gooey batter, then put the cake back in the oven. If it's clean, take out the cake and let it sit on the counter for at least 15 minutes.*

*Flip it over; hopefully, it will come out of the pan cleanly. If not, it will still taste good. If you want to ice it, you have to wait 'til it's completely cool. If the cake "fell," we call that a "sad streak," which is my favorite spot in the cake…very moist. To me that means a huge success.*

*Have fun whirring and stirring — and don't forget to lick the bowl and utensils. That's the best part!*

# The Russells: Ethel, Pug, Mama, and Sam

I've told y'all about Mamanche and Daddy Russell. They were your grandma's (my mother's) parents, your grandparents on the Russell side of the family. The best way for me to describe their four children is to talk about them from the oldest to the youngest.

The oldest was Ethel. Y'all know her extremely well today, but not in "The South I Knew." Ethel married Bill Wright and they were a jovial pair. I remember them so well when I was young. They lived in Greenville, South Carolina and had one child named Chuck, who was my age. We visited every Christmas, some Easters, every year at the beach and on our way to mountain camps. Their house was a permanent road stop for us. Greenville was a long way from Galivants Ferry back then, but we never missed the chance to visit Ethel (Aunt Effie) and her family.

Ethel and Bill were an amazing dance couple. I think dancing back in the 40s, 50s and 60s was more important than it is today. They could really 'cut a rug'; they were the best on the dance floor. I loved dancing with Uncle Bill because he was the best leader. He made me feel like I could dance too.

They would always take me to Lake Hartwell along with Chuck and my other first cousin Robert, who lived in Anderson, South Carolina. We would water ski, fish for brim, and sing silly songs. Y'all remember all those silly songs I taught you growing up? Many came from Aunt Effie. Some of those songs will be in another section near the end of the book.

I remember we'd spend the night in Greenville before driving to Brevard for my six-week summer camp at Rockbrook, a real camp with bugs in your bed and creepy crawlers everywhere!! Ethel, Chuck, Mama and Robert took me to camp many summers. These memories sparkle.

I loved visiting my cousin Chuck in Greenville, South Carolina. I remember he could act like he swallowed a basketball and his stomach was suddenly round and expansive like a huge ball was there! Seriously! And his laugh was contagious. Chuck and his family were one of my upcountry families. They took care of my brother, my sister and me when we were in college at Wolford and Converse in Spartanburg, South Carolina. I'll never forget the visits at their home when George played Godzilla with Chuck and me. He would chase us around the house until he caught us, and then he would tickle us until we thought we were dying. This makes me smile as I can almost hear him say, "GAGABUNGA!"

As you know, Chuck married his forever girlfriend Mary Anne Penland. They had two children, Chad and Lindsey. And now they have children! How did we all grow up so quickly? It only seems like yesterday Chuck was singing one of his favorite songs. "How dry I am, How wet I'll be, If I don't find the bathroom key!"

The next sibling was Aunt Pug, the organizer of the family. She married Bob Curry and lived in Anderson, South Carolina. She and Mama were roommates at Queens College in Charlotte, North Carolina before Mama transferred to the University of South Carolina. Pug and Bob had two children, Robert and Anne. You've gotten to know them especially at the reunions, so you know Robert is a Doctor in Education and Anne married and has two beautiful children, David and Shawn. You've met all of their family at The Russell Round-up!

My favorite memory in Anderson with Robert and his family included spending the night in his backyard with him and Chuck. That was when we formed a Beatles fan club. On that occasion, we did our "Beatles March" through the neighborhood. We were Beatles freaks and we wanted everyone to know how much we adored these 60's singing sensations!! We paraded through the neighborhood with banners and flags singing, "We love you Beatles, Oh yes we do. We love you Beatles and we'll be true…" We had a great time when we visited them in Anderson and when they would visit us at Myrtle Beach. Anne hung out at the beach with my brother George. They were good buddies.

The third sibling was Uncle Sam. He died when you all were young. He was a jolly Godly man who loved Christmas. One year he dressed like Santa and came to visit y'all on Christmas Eve in Galivants Ferry. It was such a treat!

Sam married a beautiful woman named Claire and they had three children: Margy, Sambo (Sam) and Bill. Bill married Rita and they have two lovely daughters, Rebecca and Brooke. You all know them well, too from the Russell Roundups and other family occasions. Their family also continues to grow with marriages and grandchildren.

As I mentioned earlier, we had many Christmas dinners with the Russells at Mamanche's house. The most vivid memories I have also are the weekends at Santee skiing, fishing, and picking the Catawba worms off the trees to use as bait. Of course, any reunion or time with the Russells included incredibly scrumptious food and lots of love.

Eventually, we began a new way of holding reunions: staging them around the opening day of dove hunting, as well as the Russell Round-ups. We still had other occasions but these two events kept us together. At the Dove hunts on opening weekend all the children of Ethel, Pug, Sam and Mama gathered together. We would have talent contests, silly song marathons, swimming parties, outdoor cooking and the famous dove meal at night. Mama, Ethel, Pug and Claire would pick up all the doves from the hunters in the field after we filled our paper sacks, take them back and make them miraculously appear for supper along with peas, butterbeans, rice, gravy, squash casserole, fresh hot biscuits, fruit salad, and broccoli casserole.

The Russell Round-up started in 1970. There was always a country meal Friday night, huge breakfast Saturday and Sunday with fresh sausage and bacon, Jenny Lou taking egg orders and all the women in the kitchen cooking up the food. We had to eat early enough so we could all go play the annual Russell Round-up golf tournament usually held at Myrtle Beach National. It was captain's choice! So that meant you could be a fair golfer and still contribute to the team. It was a big deal putting the teams together with made-up handicaps. We all had fun and somehow everyone got along even though I never ever have been on the winning team! Trophies and jokes were handed out along with crying towels. My favorite memory was when Chuck got a hole in one. I can still see the ball dropping in the cup.

On Saturday, we would go to eat at a real restaurant. The Dunes Club was a favorite along with the Sea Captain's house and Chestnut Hill. I hope you three will always keep the Russell side of your family together. It's not easy to keep up with people in this age and time but it's worth it.

Way before the actual "Russell Round-up" Chuck, Robert and I got together at the beach every summer. We started in the 50s, so the memories are hazy even to me. In those days, no one worried about being 'kidnapped' or bothered on the beach. As a result, small children we were given the freedom to wander the beach and investigate the tidal pools at dawn. There were more shells on the beach back then and we did our best to find them and bring them back to our mothers. Little did we know small animals still lived in these shells and they stunk to high heaven. We also loved to go crabbing in the swashes along the beach. These are not around us anymore.

We loved wandering the beaches alone like true explorers. There were no homes or hotels north of us, so wild sand dunes called us to explore them. We soon discovered what young couples do in the sand dunes on sandy blankets! We were extra curious about these discoveries.

Going to the Pavilion was the true highlight! The Rides, funny mirrors, the haunted house, the Bavarian Organ…The Merry go round! Roller coaster, scrambler, tilt-a-whirl…Bikini shops, the Bowery, hangouts and Bingo Parlors! The Baby rides, The Ferris wheel…What a magical afternoon or evening! You could buy tickets for very little. Each ride was a certain number of tickets. I remember those days like it was yesterday.

It's y'alls turn to carry on this family reunion and work on the other branches of our family tree!

# PART II
## My Immediate Family

# John Monroe Johnson Holliday:
# The Baby of His Family and My Daddy

John Monroe Johnson Holliday, my father and your grandfather, was a piece of work.

Daddy was the baby in his family and I was the baby in my family. He had bowed legs; I have bowed legs. He had a large head (7 5/8" to be precise) and I have the same size head. Some say the bigger your head, the smarter you are. Of course that's an old wives' tale, but even if it were true I would disagree with this premise. Instead of being smarter, I truly think it means you have the capacity to have more common sense, wisdom and discernment.

Now that doesn't mean your grandfather wasn't smart. He was extremely bright and he also had "country smarts" plus "city smarts." He could talk to anyone. He made them feel comfortable, welcome and always made time to visit with someone who just dropped by without giving any notice. He always offered them a chair, a package of nabs and a small Coca-Cola in a bottle.

Honesty with regards to all business matters was engrained in him. When daddy shook your hand, it was better than a legal "high dollar lawyer" contract. When we all sat down together and crossed our legs, he would say, "the meeting is in order." He told fellow business associates you could take his "words" to the bank. Now, no one is perfect, except God not even your granddaddy – but he tried his best to be fair to all and treat them with respect. He always started our family meetings, held every Wednesday morning with the same prayer. "Lord, let us make the right decisions for the right reason." Amen.

Daddy had lots of sayings that he loved to use. One of the more memorable I want to mention is, "I'll bet you a Pepsi-Cola." He wasn't a gambler, but when he thought he was right, he loved to win. He hated to borrow money, but sometimes he had to – especially during the beginning of the tobacco-growing season. He told everyone we had to hurry up and pay the money back to the bank 'cause "the interest grows all day and all night."

He didn't cuss much – instead he'd say, "Great Day in the Morning!" "Something's rotten in Denmark," or "What in the Helena Montana is going on." He taught Sunday school so I reckon he had to stay in practice not cussing so bad words wouldn't slip out of his mouth. He always wanted me to play *What a Friend We Have in Jesus* on the piano for church services. It wasn't until after he died that I went to the church and played the song.

His favorite joke was about brains. It goes something like this: One day, a man walked into a brain store that specialized in South Carolina College Brains. He looked at the Citadel brain and it cost $50.00. Then he noticed a University of South Carolina brain and it cost $100.00. Finally, he saw a sparkling clean Clemson brain that was so shiny he asked for its sale price. The salesman told him, "One thousand dollars." Daddy asked, "Why in the world is the Clemson brain so expensive?" The salesman said, "Because it's never been used!"

Your granddaddy laughed harder than *anyone* whenever he told this joke. I can hear his contagious laugh right now. It makes me smile.

Another favorite thing Daddy did was hand out cigarettes on "National Quit Smoking Day." He never smoked except on that one day. He'd go into banks, stores and offices of his buddies chatting, giving out free cigarettes and telling them how much healthier cigarettes were than liquor. He even said if marijuana ever became legal, he'd be the first to grow it. I'll betcha' a Pepsi Cola.

Daddy (sometimes I called him Poppa Doodle) was born and raised in Galivants Ferry. He was the baby of the third generation of Hollidays to live in this Horry County Township. I'm sure, being the baby, he was spoiled, but he grew up quickly since he was the youngest and had five sisters and a brother (he also had twin brothers who died at young ages). He was tutored at home in a little schoolhouse next to the cement tennis court. I remember it had yellow and pink small roses growing rampantly around it.

He graduated from Aynor High School and went on to be the youngest cadet ever to enter the Citadel in Charleston. It was and still is a fine military school. He went in as a skinny young boy, prospered and graduated in 1936 as a Lieutenant Colonel. He is still the youngest graduate in the Citadel's history.

He went on to teach Military History in Tennessee. During WWII, he only traveled once to Europe to bring soldiers home. I thank God that He protected Daddy.

Daddy *loved* the Citadel. It was his second home. He always said he'd attended more graduations than anyone – and my mother would add, "So have I." They always stayed at Mark Clark Hall, and I got to stay there with them when they visited me when I was a boarding student at Ashley Hall School.

Daddy was a very active member of the Citadel Alumni Association. He was a member of the Board of Visitors and a past chairman. His portrait still remains in the Citadel Library and before he died he was able to attend the grand opening of the Holliday Alumni Center, which y'all attended. I really feel God kept him alive to attend this momentous occasion. He was in rare form that evening, and with a strong voice he gave his last speech at the Citadel. Wasn't it wonderful! That memory makes me cry and smile at the same time.

Your granddaddy was sporty. He excelled in golf and tennis. Being ambidextrous, he played tennis right-handed, golf left-handed, and wrote right-handed. I don't remember how he played shuffleboard. He always dressed well and loved Brooks Brothers Clothes. Poplin or seersucker suits could carry him anywhere and he'd fit right in. He would always tell you, "When you go somewhere, carry yourself well, have confidence, and know you belong there. Talk to everyone."

He married your Grandma, which I'll discuss later. It was the best decision he ever made. For now, I want to tell you how daddy was my mentor.

Daddy loved me. I was his "Crystal Ball." I looked like him, walked like him, and talked like him. He made me feel special. I never recall him really being angry towards me or spanking me. Back in those days you "knew better" and respected your elders, especially your parents. He didn't really spoil me, even though most folks would dispute that fact. Raised by Depression-era parents, my siblings and I learned the value of a dollar. Just because I lived in a big white antebellum home, people assumed we had lots of money. I did not feel rich. I did feel richly loved by my family and the folks around me. Daddy paid me a nickel for every pair of shoes I polished, and I mowed the grass for several dollars.

Daddy's best friends called him "Monroe." He named me Christian Monroe. I became "little" Monroe to his friends, including former South Carolina Senator and Governor Fritz Hollings. That made me happy and proud. He was always home at suppertime and helped me with my history homework. He liked putting me to bed and sometimes he let me stay up pass my bedtime to watch TV, like the introduction of the Beatles on the *Ed Sullivan Show*. When I got up in the morning, we always ate breakfast together at 7 a.m.

My sister, Russell, is five years older than me, and my brother George was 10 years older. Because of the age differences, I was nearly raised as a single child and Daddy was able to spend individual time with me. He loved telling me stories of his growing up at the Ferry. He made me feel special and instilled in me a love of home.

Daddy loved the fact I played golf. Our whole family played golf together after church on Sunday afternoons. It's not proper golf etiquette to play as a five some, so I'd throw my 3-wood, 7-iron and putter in Mama's bag, run barefoot down the first hole and tee off on the second hole. The Dunes Club or Pine Lakes in Myrtle Beach were our favorite golf courses. I'll never forget paring #9 at the Dunes Club playing barefooted. It tickled him. I can hear his laughter now.

Business for Daddy was simple: Tell the truth and be fair. Your daddy says this too. If you always tell it like it is, you won't need to remember what you said. Cash was the best way to pay for everything! He wrote his own leases, contracts, and deeds. It wasn't until much later in life he switched to using lawyers. He did not want to do this at all. He hated paying lawyers especially for phone calls. He'd tell his lawyers "Don't turn that hourglass over, I just want to talk." However, times were changing and the "good ole way" of doing business and being able to trust people was sadly becoming a thing of the past.

He did, however, stick with the way he sold timber. We'd all gather in the conference room at an appointed time with timber companies. An old tobacco box with the lid that flipped open, had a hole cut in the top - a slit big enough for bids to be put on paper and slipped into this treasured box. He'd read the results, announces the winner, and that was that. Timber and tobacco put me through school. When I was young, going to tobacco market was fun. I didn't have to go, so I guess that's why it was fun. I had a choice. The auctioneers, smell of tobacco, eating a chili hotdog and visiting with the farmers made for a great day with my daddy.

I worked for Poppa after college and between marriages. He put a desk for me facing his desk. It was wonderful. I learned to love the land, our heritage and honor our traditions. The Ferry was my home, roots and future. It still is today.

As an aside I want y'all to know your granddaddy taught me songs when I was little. He was always singing, "I'm forever blowing bubbles! La de da de da de da do do. They fly so high nearly reach the sky. La de da de da de da de do!" That was all he knew from this song but he sang it a lot. It was his theme song when he wanted to go out dancing. Another song he sang all the time when I was very little was "Hush Little Baby." I want to add the whole song to this book so y'all can sing it to your own children one day. I also added in two more songs that you will certainly recall.

## Hush, Little Baby

*Hush, little baby, don't say a word.*
*Papa's gonna buy you a mockingbird*
*And if that mockingbird won't sing,*
*Papa's gonna buy you a diamond ring*

*And if that diamond ring turns brass,*
*Papa's gonna buy you a looking glass*

*And if that looking glass gets broke,*
*Papa's gonna buy you a billy goat*

*And if that billy goat won't pull,*
*Papa's gonna buy you a cart and bull*

*And if that cart and bull fall down,*
*You'll still be the sweetest little baby in town*

## Dunderbeck

*Oh Dunderbeck, Oh Dunderbeck*
*How could you be so mean?*
*To ever have invented such a terrible machine!*
*All pussy cats and long-tailed rats will never ever be seen*
*'Cause they're all ground to sausage in Dunderbeck's machine*

## A Little Boy and a Little Girl

*There was a little Boy and a little Girl*
*In an ecstasy of bliss,*
*Said the little Boy to the little Girl*
*Pray, give me just one kiss.*

*The Girl drew back in great surprise,*
*You're a stranger yet, said she.*
*And I'll give you just one kiss*
*When apples grow on a lilac tree.*

*The Boy was very sad at heart,*
*She was the only one.*
*The Girl was quite remorseful*
*At the terrible deed she had done.*

*So bright and early the very next morn*
*He was quite surprised to see*
*His little sweetheart, standing in the garden,*
*Tying apples to a lilac tree!*

# My Mama

Y'all call her "Gama."

Her real name is Marjorie Russell. She was born in Florence, South Carolina on July 19, 1920 to Mr. and Mrs. Samuel Ota Russell Sr. You three are her only grandchildren and she loves you "a bushel and a peck and a hug around the neck."

Your Grandmama is a great mother and grandmother. She was the baby of four children. In this point of the story, I want her to sit front and center. She deserves it.

Back in the earlier days, say around the 1930s through the 1960s, my opinion is that women let men get credit for just about anything except childbirth. Through my investigation of all the people I want to tell you about, I have found more information on the men than the women. I started wondering why. As I look back in my own family, my Daddy, your granddaddy, got most of the attention from his working and involvement in so many activities outside the home. There were many pictures of him. I found some of your Gama's pictures, but not as many. It dawned on me that most women take the pictures of their children, husband and events and never get their own pictures taken. Was it their choice, or was it the era? I think it was the era. So, girls, you best start posin' more.

Now, don't get me wrong. Your Gama did lots and lots and was always busy taking care of her family, her garden and her house and others at Galivants Ferry. She was active in many interests, but they were not the kind that put you in the newspaper or required portraits that hung in business halls. I want to tell you about things you might not have known some things such as she was a board member for the South Carolina Mental Institution. She could dance on roller skates, she could drink a glass water while in the middle of a full back bend and she did this on Broadway! There were also many events for which your Gama was responsible in my life and yours.

Mama's nickname was "Gunsmoke." That meant she was in charge of our family and you better listen to her or else. She was very kind and I rarely remember her raising her voice, but she meant business and got things done.

She and Jenny Lou made sure we had balanced meals, which meant something yellow, something green and a protein of some sort...and always bread and dessert. Every meal was planned out and we always ate at the same time of day when possible. The food was fresh. Her vegetables came from "Margy's Garden" and the fish came from "Margy's Pond."

She was there at night for us and usually every afternoon unless she was playing golf or having bridge club. She had lots of friends from Myrtle Beach, Mullins, Marion, Florence, and of course Galivants Ferry. The people around the Ferry knew if they needed anything, she would get it to them. She made sure her extended families were doing well. Willie Murrow said, "Ms. Margie was always nice to everyone. If you needed anything she would help you."

She was good at golf and averaged a 20 handicap. I loved playing with her and her Dunes Club women. She was also a heck of a good dancer. Daddy was, too. They used to take dancing lessons and they got the crowd's attention when they got up to cha-cha. She was social in the fact that she and Daddy were members of lots of dance clubs, many golf clubs and kept up with all the folks in towns surrounding Galivants Ferry.

A good woman is hard to find but Daddy found Mama. They met at the Pavilion in Myrtle Beach. She was engaged to someone else and had to return the engagement ring. Due to family differences, she and Daddy eloped. Her mother Mamanche put her on the train in Florence and sent her off to Charleston to marry your granddaddy. They were married with Sally Chapman, one of Mama's best friends, as a witness and the Haygoods looking on as well. I know Mama would have loved a big wedding but she and daddy were so in love this suited them fine.

After marriage they lived in Charleston in a drafty apartment. The holes between the floor slats were wide enough to see the neighbors below. Daddy taught Political Science at the Citadel. Then they moved several times and lived in Mullins in the Bishop Anderson apartments. She had her first born, George, during this period. These were happy times.

She was a great, supportive wife. She had three children: George, Russell, and me. We were spaced about five years apart, so there was a big difference in the ages.

When I was 13, Mama's only son George was killed in a car accident in Inman, South Carolina on November 1, 1967. This tore the heart and soul out of your Grandma. I was told she would not come out of the house for a long time. I guess I have shut out a lot of the memories. She had always centered herself around your granddaddy, but now she had two children left. She was depressed and did not want to do anything. So, even though your granddaddy was also destroyed, he was able to focus on his steady daily business...and his eyes turned elsewhere. Daddy needed hugs, and Mama did not have them. They never ever let us know anything was going on. They never had quarrels out loud. After years, things calmed down, and your Gama forgave your granddaddy. I am not sure I could have done that. I admire her strength and commitment to our family. She took care of him for the rest of his life.

Okay...let's skip to happier thoughts. Mama always made sure birthdays, Valentines, all holidays, and Christmases were extra special. She oversaw everything. Even New Year's Day meals were tradition. In the South on New Year's Day, you either ate proper foods or the New Year was jinxed. You had to have pork of some kind, black-eyed peas, or field peas and greens. Do y'all remember what they stood for? Pass this on to your own families because it's important...Pork (we had what you call greasy rice made from backbone and rice) represented a healthy year ahead. Peas insured you of a lucky year, and the Greens meant you were going to have a good financial year. Why in the world would you want to chance fate?

My nickname is little Monroe and I do look like your granddaddy, but I learned all these Mama type things from your Gama. She deserves the credit for the traditions I instilled in all of you as you grew up. Daddy added a bunch, too, but I wanted you all to know where the nesting part of your life comes from.

There are many wonderful activities Mama introduced me to. We shopped twice a year in Charleston. She was a beautifully dressed woman and she wanted her children dressed well, too. She instilled in me the desire to look my best. I reckon that is why y'all like to shop.

Mama taught me to fish and catch crabs. These are special memories for me. We enjoyed fishing at home and at the beach. Y'all know the pond behind our house is called "Margy's Pond." Back then no one could out fish Mamma in her pond or surf fishing. It takes just the right feel to catch brim or bass on a cane pole with a tiny hook and a lively cricket. At the beach she taught me how to catch sand fiddlers for fresh bait. You could catch a mess of whiting with these critters. She taught me everything I know.

Going crabbing was special. We enjoyed this activity with two of her best friends, TD Steadman, and Kitty Lou Tilgham. They had wonderful places to catch large pots of fresh blue crabs. We were all buddies then and age did not seem to matter. We just had fun together.

Do y'all remember how you learned to crab in Garden City? Do you remember it took "the magic touch?" Well, I learned this delicate touch skill from grandma and I taught it to y'all. Just like fishing you've got to feel the little tugs, set the hook or in this case scoop the crab in a net. This is an art. I think we even used Mama's old crabsticks and attached twine and fish heads to them. The stinkier the better. Nothing was better than catching 'dem blue crabs in a creek, tossing them in a straw basket and picking them for supper. A Southern delicacy for sure and southern skill passed down from generation to generation. Learning to pluff love mud and losing your tennis shoes is a very pleasant memory, too.

Oh, I'll never forget how Mama described the demise of the crabs as "we're just putting them to sleep" while putting them in a huge pot of boiling water. To this day, that pot is at the beach house along with the same crab lines made out of heavy painter's stirrers, large hooks and heavy weight. She was saving them for y'all.

Mama also instilled in me a love for golf. We played in all the women's groups all over. Her friends were my friends, too. That's the way it worked! I remember when grandma and I used to put a cricket box and two poles in our golf bags when we played at the Dunes Club. On hole #6 if we were not playing well, we'd just quit and go fishing. We'd let the other golfers play through. Golf etiquette and bream fishing went had in hand. Fun recollection!!

Grandma and the chickens made wonderful memories, too. All the chickens in her chicken yard knew her. She fed them table scraps every day and they'd run to greet her at her first call of "here chicky, chicky, chicky!" They loved laying eggs for her, too. Bright yellow sunny side eggs on toast were a morning ritual. No cholesterol either. Her chickens liked her so much they let her pick them up sometimes. She could even help them go to sleep. I think you've seen this before. Instructions; first you hold the chicken gently, tuck its head under one of its arms (wing). Then, holding the chicken with both hands make a large oval circle with your arms swinging the hen 'til you can tell she's relaxed, lay her on the ground and she is truly asleep, unhurt and napping. I promise it works. Try it the next time you come home!

Gama also loved working in the yard. Who do you think kept up her huge yard? Mama did with the help from William Murrow, JW Davis and others but Mama was the "Gunsmoke" behind her beautiful yard. So, now this love for yards has passed on to me! It's hard work and you can't keep long nails but the results are so worth it!

Your Gama still lives next door, and she is now 91 years old. She was very active 'til your granddaddy died. Lots of people have kept her going and she is still funny, happy and loving. As you remember, she even had a 'friend' after daddy died. Mr. Martin Barringer helped Mama a lot. We never guessed he would pass before Mama.

It appears Gama doesn't remember a lot, but she is happy and pleasant. Yesterday, she told me she loved me. She loves you all so much. You are her three boo-boos. Y'all know she played golf until several years ago and she surprised us by played the piano not very long ago. She still knows people who love her.

When you come home, spend as much time as you can with her. You may not think so, but she knows every moment you are there. I thank God every day for giving us such a loving Mama and grandmama. She taught the whole family The Golden Rule. Y'all know how important this rule is! Do unto others, as you would have them do unto you. Or as your Gama would say, "Hold 'em in the road."

# My Favorites from My Mama

Here are some of Mama's recipes and songs that I want y'all to remember.

## Congo Squares (or Missionary Squares if you use butterscotch)
- 1 package of sweet chocolate chips or caramel chips
- 1 and 1/3 stick butter melted
- 1 lb. light brown sugar
- 3 Eggs
- 2¾ cups sifted flour
- 2½ tsp baking powder
- ½ tsp salt
- 1 tsp vanilla

*Melt butter, stir in brown sugar, and then stir in the sifted flour. Add the beaten eggs to batter. Mix the baking powder and the salt in well. Mix all together well and add 1 package of sweet chocolate chips or caramel chips.*

*Add 1 cup chopped nuts if desired. Add 1 tsp vanilla. Cook 350 degrees for 27 minute in a 10 x 15 inch pan. Do not overcook! They also freeze well.*

## Christmas Cookie Mix to Leave Out for Santa
- 1 2 lb. cake flour
- 2 ¼ cups bread flour
- 1/3 cup baking powder
- 1 TBS salt
- 8 cups sugar
- 3 cups of shortening

*Sift dry ingredients two times. Cut in shortening, store in airtight container. Then, to make the cookies:*
- 3 cups mix
- 1 egg
- ¼ tsp. nutmeg
- 1 tsp. vanilla

*Chill then roll out dough and then cut out with cookie-cutters. Bake at 350 until brown.*

## Margy's Prune Cake

- *2 cups sugar*
- *2 cups self-rising flour*
- *1 tsp nutmeg*
- *1 tsp allspice*
- *1 tsp cinnamon*
- *1 cup chopped nuts*
- *2 or 3 eggs*
- *1 cup Mazola oil*
- *1 jar junior size baby prunes*

*Mix all together and put in Bundt cake pan. Bake 50 to 60 minutes at 350 degrees.*

## Backbone and Rice: For Prosperity & Health on New Year's Day

- *2 pounds pork backbones*
- *6 cups water*
- *1 1/2 teaspoons salt*
- *2 teaspoon pepper*
- *2 cups uncooked rice*

*Bring first 4 ingredients to a boil in a large pot over medium-high heat. Cover, reduce heat to low, and simmer, stirring occasionally, 1 1/2 hours or until meat is tender.*

*Stir in rice; cover and cook over low heat 20 to 25 minutes or until rice is done. (Do not stir.) Fluff rice with a fork, and serve. (Alternate for wimps: Pork Tenderloin)*

## Black Eyed Peas: For Luck on New Year's Day

- *2 pounds dried black-eyed peas*
- *8 ounces hog jowl or 2 small to medium ham hocks*
- *6 cups water*
- *1 large onion, coarsely chopped*
- *1/2 teaspoon crushed red pepper*
- *1/4 teaspoon sugar*
- *Salt to taste*

*Pick over the peas and rinse well, then soak in cold water overnight. Place ham hocks or hog jowl in large kettle with water, bring to boil, and cook for 1 1/2 hours. Drain peas and add to the hog jowl.*

*Add whole onion, crushed red pepper, sugar, and salt. Add more water if needed to cover peas. Cover tightly and simmer slowly 2 hours or until peas are tender. Serve with hot cooked rice and cornbread. Serves 8.*

## Southern Collard Greens
- *1 1/2 quarts water*
- *1 1/2 pounds ham hocks*
- *4 pounds collard greens, rinsed and trimmed*
- *1/2 teaspoon crushed red pepper flakes (optional)*
- *1/4 cup vegetable oil*
- *Salt and pepper to taste*

*Place the water and the ham hock in a large pot with a tight-fitting lid. Bring to a boil. Lower the heat to very low and simmer covered for 30 minutes. Add the collards and the hot pepper flakes the pot. Simmer covered for about 2 hours, stirring occasionally. Add the vegetable oil and simmer covered for 30 minutes.*

### ###

And here are a couple of songs that my Mama used to sing. I want to add the whole song to this letter so y'all can sing it to your own children one day.

## Jenny Made Her Mind Up
Jenny made her mind up when she was three
She herself was going to trim the Christmas tree
Christmas Eve she lit the candles, tossed the tapers away
Little Jenny was an orphan on Christmas day

Poor Jenny, bright as a penny
Her equal would be hard to find
She lost one dad and mother, a sister and a brother,
But she would make up her mind

Jenny made her mind up when she was twelve
That into foreign languages she would delve
But at seventeen to Vassar, it was quite a blow
That in twenty-seven languages she couldn't say no
Poor Jenny, bright as a penny
Her equal would be hard to find
To Jenny I'm beholden, her heart was big and golden
But she would make up her mind

Jenny made her mind up at twenty-two
To get herself a husband was the thing to do
She got herself all dolled up in her satins and furs
And she got herself a husband--but he wasn't hers

Poor Jenny, bright as a penny
Her equal would be hard to find
Deserved a bed of roses, but history discloses
That she would make up her mind

Jenny made her mind up at fifty-one
She would write her memoirs before she was done
The very day her book was published, history relates,
There were wives who shot their husbands in some thirty-three states

Jenny made her mind up at seventy-five
She would live to be the oldest woman alive
But gin and rum and destiny play funny tricks,
And poor Jenny kicked the bucket at seventy-six
Jenny points a moral with which you cannot quarrel,
Makes a lot of common sense--Jenny and her saga prove that you're gaga
If you don't keep sitting on the fence

Jenny and her story point the way to glory
To all man and womankind
Anyone with vision comes to this decision--
Don't make up your mind

## A Bushel and a Peck
I love you a bushel and peck
A bushel and peck and a hug around the neck
A hug around the neck and a barrel and a heap
A barrel and a heap and I'm talking in my sleep about you, about you

Cause I love you a bushel and a peck
You bet your pretty neck, I do
I love you a bushel and peck
A bushel and peck though you make my heart a wreck
Make my heart a wreck and you make my life a mess
Make my life a mess, yes
A mess of happiness, about you, about you

'Cause I love you a bushel and a peck, You bet your pretty neck, I do
I love you a bushel and peck, a bushel and peck and it beats me all to heck
Beats me all to heck and I'll never tend the farm
Never tend the farm when I wanna keep my arm
About you, about you

# George: My Brother, Your Uncle

I am not sure how to start this letter.

It's so hard to believe, even now, that my children never met my brother, your uncle George. You would have loved him. He was a tall, good looking brunette. He looked like your Gama. His eyes were dark brown and they had a sparkle, especially when he was smiling, which was most of the time. He got along with all kinds of people and could talk to anyone. Even though he was 10 years older than me, I still felt close to him. He would let me spy on him and hang around him and his friends (even his girlfriends every once in a while.)

He loved the Ferry. He had a red go-cart and rigged it so it would go especially fast around the house and down the driveway. We might still have that go-cart. Hunting and playing golf were his favorite activities, but his talent at playing golf was extraordinary. His handicap was a plus-1, which is very, very good. He played in tournaments all over the area. There is a scrapbook at the store with all his newspaper clippings if you ever want to look at them. Some of his other favorite pastimes included playing pool and baseball with his buddies in Galivants Ferry

I remember many nights; he would have guys over playing pool and records in the Big Play House. Mama's front yard was their baseball field, and a broken window was not uncommon. George was also crazy about having people go to our Myrtle Beach house. He would go to the Beach Club (the "in" spot for listening to musicians like The Drifters, The Tams, Swinging Medallions and Major Lance, just to name a few) and somehow bring the stars back to the beach house. I loved spying on these crowds. You can imagine how jumping from the living room floor of a split level house over the opening to the play room and landing on the counter top in the dining room might be dangerous. They did this. One night, a person actually landed on his knees and made a dent in the counter. They had good clean fun and I watched.

George took time to be with me. Those times were so special for me. He took time to give me golf lessons, play putt-putt, go to movies and teach me how to put topspin, back spin, and sidespin on pool balls. Everyone needs to be able to handle a cue stick and know how to cut the pool balls, play position and have a solid break. George made sure his sisters could stand their own against any male player.

One year, George drove my sister Russell and me to school every day. He was a prankster and loved making us do silly things. When it was hot, George would roll all the windows up in his car, turn on the heat as high as it would go and see how long we could stand it. It would destroy our hairdos before we would get to school; that drove us crazy. When it was freezing outside, he would turn the AC as cold as possible. At least the cold did not mess your hair up. One day, a dead hog was lying in the road. He stopped the car, and we had to touch it before he would take us to school. We were tardy a lot, but it was worth it.

George went off to college in '63. Your granddaddy wanted him to go to the Citadel so he and his best friend Butch Smith headed to the military school in Charleston, SC Freshmen were called knobs, which seems appropriate considering what they had to go through at the Citadel. George and Butch checked into their barracks got their heads shaved, stayed awake all night from fear — and returned home the next day. So much for being a Citadel cadet. Your granddaddy was on the Citadel Board of Visitors and all the upper classmen knew this fact, so they were ready for Col. John Monroe Holliday's son. Hazing at the Citadel was in fashion, so George and Butch had every right to be scared to death.

Your grandmama was thrilled to get her baby home.

Next was Furman University in Greenville, where he finished his first freshman semester and then transferred to Wofford College in Spartanburg, SC He joined the Kappa Sigma fraternity and was happy as a clam. He met the love of his life, Marianne Sagar, and they were 'pinned', which means he gave his Kappa Sigma pin to her — a pre-engagement. Your Aunt Russell entered Converse College, which was right down the road in the same town. Life was perfect. Meanwhile, I was in the 8th grade at Mullins High School living a full life of adolescent bliss.

On Halloween night 1967, George and three classmates took George's car on a road trip to Mt. Mitchell in the North Carolina Mountains several hours above Spartanburg to witness the first snowfall of the year. Your Uncle George loved weather and wanted to be a meteorologist. His room at home was covered with weather news clippings. He loved snow.

On Nov. 1 in the wee hours of the morning, while headed back for morning classes, George's car hit an overpass on I-26 near Inman, South Carolina. They were all killed. A woman heard the crash and ran to help, only to find looters at the site. She was able to determine your uncle was in the back seat, not driving, and probably asleep when the glass window cut his throat, killing him instantly. That was good to know, in that he did not suffer. I do not know the details of how the other boys died, but my heart continues to ache for their families.

The memories of November 1, 1967 are still crystal clear. When we found out hours after the crash, Mama was at the beauty parlor, Daddy was at work, Russell was at Converse College, and I was in Mullins High School. It feels like yesterday. I was called out of Mrs. Granthem's room while she was beginning to administer a test to the class. The mimeographed test papers had been handed out as we sat in our wooden desks, and then I was called over the loud speaker to come to the principal's office — a scary thought to begin with. I had a test to take. I did not trick or treat the night before so I could study. What was going on? I was called to the principal's office.

Walking down the high ceiling dark hallway, I noticed two of my best friends, Jane and Harriett, huddled together staring at me. Why were they out of class? Billy Holliday, a first cousin from Galivants Ferry, appeared inside the main doors of the school. He had come to get me. Why? He never picked me up from school.

We got in his car...silence. I asked him why he was picking me up when I had a test to take. More silence. His eyes were red and moist. He held himself together for the 15-minute drive to the Ferry, which seemed like forever. As we drove in the curving driveway of my home, he stopped halfway. He looked at me and said, "Be strong, Christy. It'll be alright." I'm not sure if he hugged me, but I could feel his love and deep sadness.

Bursting into the den, I hollered, "What's going on! " Someone took me upstairs to my parents' bedroom. The room was not well lit. Mama and Daddy looked through me. I could see their pain and sadness. They were scared to say what they had to say. "George was in a wreck, Christy. He died."

I went nuts. "NO, NO, NO. It can't be true. There has got to be a mistake. It wasn't George. We need to see for ourselves. Whoever spread this rumor was wrong! I don't believe you."

I wanted proof. George *had* to be alive. This could not possibly be happening to us. Things like this happened in other families, but not ours!

But it was true. As the reality hit. I went to bed.

That night, George comforted me. He came to my bedside, sat on the bed, and told me it would be Okay. My sister and I had identical dreams a few days later. We feel George was telling us he was fine and for us to not be troubled and we had to keep going.

The funeral was massive. It was held on a bright sunny day in the front yard where George played baseball. In keeping with old Southern tradition, George spent the night before the funeral in an open casket in the living room. His favorite cat Ashley slept on his casket. She was the last thing he kissed when he left home for the final time. Ever a tenderhearted boy and man, he had even turned around to come back to kiss her because he had forgotten.

A cavalcade of cars lined up for the 15-mile ride from Galivants Ferry to Rose Hill Cemetery in Marion. The line appeared to be endless. As I gazed out of the rear window of the hearse, you could not see the end of the line of cars. We buried George, said our goodbyes after the funeral and drove back home. His headstone has snowflakes carved around it, each snowflake different, as they are in nature. The details of his last trip to see snow and his life are also engraved on the top.

This is not a happy story, but it's one I needed to tell you. I want you three to love each other like there won't be a tomorrow. You never know when God will take you from this life. I am sure one day you all will meet George. You will like him a lot, but watch out, 'cause I bet he is still a prankster. He loves to hold kids down and tickle them and play like he is Godzilla…gagabunga! It'll be fun.

Life goes on and we all recover in different ways. Getting over bad stuff is never easy, and each individual does it their way. Aunt Russell went back to Converse, Marian graduated from Converse and moved to California, I went off to Ashley Hall, a boarding school in Charleston, Daddy submerged himself in business and a multitude of activities, and Mama took a while to re-emerge, but she survived and started back working in the yard and playing golf. Back then, no one went to therapists. At least we didn't. You just went forward. I would not recommend this method. You have to deal with trauma, death, or whatever as soon as possible or it will hang onto you like an albatross.

This is another reason I had to tell you three this story. You must take care of yourselves and reach out to friends, family or professionals if you need help. Love one another and be there for each other.

# My Seester: Marjorie Russell Holliday Jr.

Y'all call her Aunt Russell.

When she lived in New York City, she was referred to as Auntie Russell, a reference to *Mame*, the Broadway play. She was not going to be called "big Russell" under any circumstances. Even though I named my second daughter "little Russell" after her, if we had called her big Russell, I think she would have issued a decree to get everyone to call you Marjorie – end of subject.

She was named after your grandmother, hence the Jr. I like to tell everyone I am the youngest sister, but everyone thinks I am the oldest, which means you children have made me age faster than my seester. Shame on y'all. Why do I call her seester? I really don't remember, but it is stuck in my head, so that's my nickname for her. (I think it had something to do with one of our scuba diving trips to Mexico, so the accent was Mexican).

Your Aunt Russell was born July 11, 1949; she's five years older than me. Back then; it must have been the trend to spread babies out, since your Uncle George was another five years older than her. Due to this age difference, I was considered the pesky little sister. I'll never, ever forget her playing on the piano: "Christy is a baby/Christy is a baby." They say sticks and stones may break bones and words won't hurt, but these lyrics drove me crazy. She won all the arguments and fights we had by singing this song, 'cause I would lose my cool. I would run to tattle on her to Jenny Lou or Mama, "Make her quit!!!" It never worked. She could hum it and still make me nuts.

One night, your grandmama left all the kids with granddaddy. He was not used to being a baby sitter, so he let us do what we wanted. He was just not equipped to keep an eye on George, Russell and me at the same time. As you might expect, accidents happened. George had a party in the big playhouse shooting pool with his local friends. Beer and cigarettes left everywhere. Russell and I were playing upstairs, which was really more like "fighting." We were having an innocent pillow fight – the serious kind; the I'm-going-to-hurt-you kind – and she won by once again humming that same old song. Since she was taller and bigger than me, her pillow hit an old brass lamp with a broken thick glass shade, which fell and sliced my thigh wide open. Blood was gushing out and we just stared each other wide-eyed, ran into our parents' bathroom and tried to stop the flow of the red yucky fluid.

It wasn't working 'til one of us remembered from Girl Scouts the word 'tourniquet'. We stopped the flow and hollered downstairs to Daddy. "We think we need a doctor, Daddy!"

Scared, we both knew the cut was really deep and we think we saw a bone and white corpuscle type things in the gash. We ended up at the emergency room in Mullins, a nearby town, and I got stitched up with 11 stitches, even though the wound probably needed twice that and on two levels. That is why the scar on my leg today is so big and ugly. Let this be a lesson to y'all. Do not let your kids have pillow fights unless you are the referee.

Later in life, we got along much better. I grew to be old enough and good enough shooting pool for her to ask me to be her accomplice in pool hall bars at the beach. We frequented places like Donnie's at Cherry Grove, the Spanish Galleon in Ocean Drive and the Magic Carpet on Highway 17 at Windy Hill. Russell was and still is a beautiful woman. She had a dark tan, long blonde hair, and the guys would flock around her. She would quietly ask them with a flirty tone, "Y'all want to play a couple of games with my little sister and me?" They would laugh and accept her offer. Then we took their money.

As we got older, sneaking out of our Myrtle Beach home became the thing to do. Neither one of us knew the other was sneaking out. So, one night we ran into each other in the beach house yard. Surprised, Russell asked me, "What are you doing out here?" "I'm sneaking out," I replied matter-of-factly. "What are you doing?"

"How did you get out?"

"Out the front door. How did you get out?"

She said, "I climbed out my bedroom window!"

That was the last time she climbed out the window. From then on, we were a twosome. We'd sneak out a door, get daddy's Cadillac, push it out of the garage and a little down the street, and crank it up. Off we went to Ocean Drive. That's where the cool people went to shag, the South Carolina's state dance. We had good clean fun. Seriously, we would come back way before dawn. We never got caught.

(By the way, I am telling you this since it's too late for y'all to sneak out anymore, but I want you to know I was aware of everything you all have done or at least most of it. Watch out for your own children, 'cause what goes around comes around!)

Your Aunt Russell went off to College, and the next time we were living in the same city was during my Ashley Hall Senior year in Charleston. She had graduated from Converse College in Spartanburg and became a teacher at First Baptist School. It was super having a sister with an apartment not far from me in the coolest city, The Holy City, the nickname for Charleston. With so many fun things to do and a place for overnights, I was "In like Flynn", and all my friends were, too.

Eventually, New York City called her. She answered the call and moved to the Big Apple. With no experience, she was able to talk her way into several business positions. First, she got a job on Wall Street with Morgan Stanley. Then a job putting a magazine together for NASCAR. (She knew absolutely nothing about this sport or putting magazines together). Next, she hopped over to *Redbook* and eventually *Town and Country*. She was a New Yorker with a nice co-op on east 79th, neat NYC friends, long red fingernails, and high-fashion clothes. She loved having your daddy and I for visits. She would hold her Christmas party and we would bring up famous South Carolina BBQ and Jenny Lou's biscuits. How neat having an uptown sister in New York City!

Eventually, New York lost its sparkle for Russell, and she moved back home. She sold her co-op, which I still think was a huge mistake, and bought a house in Myrtle Beach on the 9th tee at the Dunes Club. She came back to learn our family business and meet a Southern fellow to marry. A Yankee would not fit in Galivants Ferry.

But first, I married your Daddy. Aunt Russell was my only maid of honor (for the second time, since this was my second marriage). Not so long after that, maybe a few years, while your Daddy and I were living in Greenville, we went on a dove hunt and I met Hal Cottingham. As usual, I was on the look for available men, discovered he was single and told him he had to "meet my sister."

They met and eventually married. Hal still says she had dated every potential man in South Carolina and he was her last chance. I am not sure about that, but she had been through a bunch. Several guys, after hearing that Hal and Russell were not living together after the nuptials, in particular Joe McVay said, "If I had known I did not have to live with her, I would have married her a long time ago."

Your aunt is a modern-day "keep your maiden name" woman. She is the Queen of Galivants Ferry and I am the princess. You all can be the Ladies and Lord in waiting.

Of course, Grandma is still the Queen Mother.

# My Jenny Lou

"Spider's hot! How you want 'dem eggs?"

This is what I heard just about every morning growing up in Galivants Ferry. The spider was part of the stove eyes. Jenny Lou could cook like no one you've ever known. She didn't use recipes. She couldn't read, and didn't even know how old she was. She didn't need to know, 'cause it did not matter. My whole family loved her and she was family. She raised me, like Aretha has helped raise you kids.

Jenny Lou was a petite lady, about 5 feet 3 inches, small boned, with twinkling eyes, a big ole' smile and long arms to reach out and hug you even when you didn't feel like it. She wore a uniform every day. I don't recall seeing her in anything but a white starched dress with a white apron and a matching white cap. She loved her snuff, and you always knew where you stood with her. She did not hold her tongue.

Even though she couldn't read, I believe she taught me some of the best life lessons not only by telling me stories but also by her actions. She expressed her love. She told people she loved them. She treated everyone the same, no matter whether it was fancy company coming to visit Mama and Daddy or my friends or people driving through the yard. She was wise, too. Her gut intuition could tell bad people from good people, so if she thought anyone was not quite right, she would not open the door. She read people like some people read a book. She read people with her heart. She taught me to tell the truth, and that little white lies were just as bad as big 'uns. She always used the expression, "truth be known." Only recently did I find out that the phrase comes straight from the Bible. She knew the Bible, even though she could not read it. She was a good Christian lady, inside and out.

One of the most vivid memories of Jenny Lou comes from the 60s. Those were turbulent times, but I did not know it even though it surrounded me. Things looked the same to me and life went on like normal. Jenny Lou kept me lots of the time. We watched our "stories" like *The Edge of Night* and *All My Children*. She put me to bed at night and we said our prayers together. I never once thought our skin colors were different.

Those were the years of change. I was born in 1954, so I was too young to pay attention to the news or read the newspaper (or it was kept from me). Life went on as normal. Jenny Lou cooked and took care of my sister, my brother and me. One thing perplexed me, though: why wouldn't she sit at the table with us and eat with us? Also, she drank out of a mason jar. I remember trying to get her to sit down, but she wouldn't listen to me. She sat on a stool in the kitchen with a swinging door. If Daddy or Mama called her, she would be there to refill or re-serve their plates...and mine. Jenny Lou acted like this was normal so I went along with the order of things even though I did not understand it.

One night, while were staying at Myrtle Beach, we decided to go to the picture show. We invited Jenny Lou to join us, so that meant we would go to the picture show theatre in Ocean Drive. They had a "colored" section. There was a separate entrance with a narrow stairway that led up to the balcony. I went with Jenny Lou. Up there, you could smoke cigarettes. Jenny Lou did not smoke, but she carried her snuff with her. We had fun together. Dipping snuff was ok and much better than cigarette smoke. You put a pinch of snuff in your jowl area and kept it there to enjoy the flavor, and they say it has nicotine in it, which is enjoyable. I did not mind. I just liked being able to watch the movie with her.

All my friends loved Jenny Lou, too. If y'all go up to any of my Mullins friends today they can tell you so many stories about her. She kept an eye on all of us at the same time. She was a great baby sitter, chaperone for overnights, and when we had pool parties or big playhouse parties she was there, but you just did not see her. She knew we were playing 'spin the bottle', 'choo-choo' and other adolescent games while we listened to the Beatles on the record player. Our hormones were jumping around at that time in our lives but Jenny Lou knew that was normal and let us get away with it 'cause she knew it was normal and we weren't old enough to really get into trouble. We were just sticking our toes in the water.

At the beach, there was – and still is – a "colored beach." Atlantic Beach is located between Myrtle Beach and Windy Hill. The beach is actually cut off from the other beaches by fences that stretch over dunes; no roads connected it with the other beaches. I need to go down there and see if it's still the same. I hope it's different now.

Y'all know I am not prejudiced at all; so using these terms makes me jittery because I do not really talk like this, but to get the point across, I have to tell you the way people used to talk. Anyway, back to the story…Mama or Daddy and I used to take Jenny Lou and a friend to Atlantic Beach. I'm sure my sister and brother did the same since they could drive and I could not. Atlantic Beach was a hot spot. You could tell the people were happy-go-lucky. I wanted to go, too. No one ever told me why I could not go, but I guess I was too young and too white. Plus, Jenny Lou needed time with her buddies.

I have lots of stories, but some stick out more than others. I am not sure I have told you this one, but I promise it's the truth and I remember it like it was yesterday. One afternoon, I was swimming in our pool (which we called the cement pond) and a young black boy asked if he could join me. I think he was kin to Jenny Lou.

"Sure!" I said. He jumped in to play with me.

In two seconds flat, Jenny Lou opened the screen door of the kitchen and yelled as loud as she could as she stormed towards the pool, "Get out of 'dat water…you look like a fly in a bowl of milk!"

It scared me as much as it did him. What had we done wrong?

Jenny Lou had many specialties, but her finest was Southern cooking…yet she stayed so thin! She and your Grandmama had a garden behind the stables. She and Mama, plus your great grandma Mamanche, put up vegetables all late spring, summer and fall…we had a freezer full. (Honestly, I never ate any canned vegetables while growing up in Galivants Ferry) Many of your kinfolk helped them plant the garden. Some of the vegetables Jenny Lou would pick early in the morning included silver queen white corn, baby butter beans, field peas, squash, string beans, okra and mustard greens, to name a few. Delicious!

Jenny Lou and Mama made sure we put up enough for a whole year 'til the next planting. Jenny Lou knew how to cook all of these and she was famous for her meals. No one ever left the table hungry when she was around. She made homemade biscuits, cooked "bagetti" (spaghetti), rump roasts and fried chicken. Since we were so close to the beach, her fried seafood platters were better than going to any of the seafood restaurants around the beach.

I want to give y'all some of her recipes. She taught me how to cook them and I have cooked them for y'all but you need the ingredients, since nothing is written down. Before I start pulling the recipes out of my head, I want to tell you again just how much Jenny Lou meant to all of us. She made me realize "we" are no better than others. We all came in to this world the same way. The color of your skin does not matter, nor should it. She loved me like Aretha loved y'all. We are blessed to have such special people in our lives.

## Jenny Lou's Rump Roast

- *2 tablespoons oil*
- *3 medium onions chopped*
- *1 4-pound rump roast*
- *Water*
- *Salt and pepper to taste*
- *¼ cup plain flour*

*Heat oil in 5-quart Dutch oven over medium heat. Liberally salt and pepper roast. Brown roast very slowly for 20 minutes, turning occasionally to brown evenly. Add chopped onions and cook for 10 minutes. Add enough water to cover half the roast.*

*Cover and continue to cook over medium heat for 2 ½-3 hours or until tender. Check roast occasionally to make sure it does not stick, adding enough water to keep meat half covered.*

*When tender, remove roast to platter and let grave cool slightly. Make a paste with flour and ½ cup water. Stir paste with fork until very smooth. Stir an additional 2 cups water into paste and blend well. Slowly add flour mixture to warm gravy and bring to a boil.*

*Return roast to pan, cover and simmer for 30 minutes. Remove the roast from pan and slice. To serve, arrange slice of roast on plaster and top with gravy.*

*This meal goes great with mustard greens, rice, squash casserole, butter beans, fried okra, fried chicken and homemade biscuits (or the frozen ones). Ain't nothin' better than dipping a biscuit in gravy!*

# PART III
## The Fabric of Galivants Ferry

# A Tapestry of Southern Charm

For generations, the people of Galivants Ferry have woven together to create a rich tapestry of Southern culture and history. That's why this place is so special.

People, like fabrics, have different make-ups: soft cotton, itchy wool, that stretchy 60s fabric, smooth silk, thick corduroy, intricate damask...the list never ends. The weave brings together things that don't usually match, whether through knitting, cross-stitching, embroidery, basting, needlepointing and machine made. As with people, mistakes are a given, so the fabric of the Ferry might have a few dropped stitches and a few holes while the other parts have been exquisitely detailed. The measurements might be off at times, so the widths may vary.

Southerners, in my opinion, are friendlier than most. They speak to you without being spoken to. They take care of their own. Perhaps some think we are too personal, but we can't help it. There are nice Southerners and not so nice Southerners. There are very honest folks and little white lie folks. We hold the past close to our hearts and our emotions run deep (one result of the War of the Northern Aggression). We are not the prejudiced people most would have you believe. From my perspective, we are sometimes more forgiving than perhaps we should be.

Put it all together, and you have the uniqueness that is found here in this tightly woven township. You could compare it to an old quilt made from the colorful kinfolk that have given Galivants Ferry its character in the five generations my family has called this place home.

I want y'all to know that even though times will continue to change, it is important to honor, respect and hold dear your ancestry. We all came into this world the same way, and ain't nobody better than the other fellow. The way you live your life and how you treat others is up to you.

# I Love Being a Southerner in a Small Town

Y'all know even though lots of memorabilia of the Old South is gone, there is still enough left to wet your whistle for the old times.

There are mules, cows, sheep, goats and many other barnyard and chicken yard critters scattered about. There are tobacco barns and pack houses of many past eras still being utilized, even though they are about to fall down in some instances. However, the largest group and most colorful genre of the Old South are the people themselves. I reckon you can count me as part of this crowd cause it's in my core.

Most of these folks are hospitable and super friendly. That's the best way to describe them. We could call them the "HEY, HOW Y'ALL" people. Wherever you go in the true South, a nod of your head or a small wave of your hand from your steering wheel as you pass others means "hey y'all" or "howdy" or "see you later." In other words, it means whatever you meant to say or whatever the recipient took it to mean.

Many feelings have been hurt due to the absence of these small gestures of communication. You just can't ignore people on country roads or stores. It's considered downright unfriendly. My Mama used to say, "They don't know no better."

Down in the South, you speak to just about everyone. You might know them or you might not. They might know you and even your name, so you might need some acting skills to speak back like you remember them. Getting older does not help with the memory skills, but acting nice is a born trait.

Just today I was in a small country store, a post office, bank, and a gun store. Quite a combination, huh? Anyway, everyone spoke to everyone. They truly either knew each other or acted like they did. People spoke about "so and so's" stepmother who had cancer and could not walk to the mailbox, and someone finally put her in the hospital, and why did it take them so long to admit her? Everyone around added their concerns and opinions. We call it "their two cents worth of advice." There were whispers 'bout who was seeing whom and so glad they were happy now. The juicy details were really whispered quietly.

In general, people talk to you and act like they really know you, which is a warm feeling. It might be a little like make-believe, and some think you ought to say something like, "I know we have met but I can't remember your name." No, no…don't do this. It's not worth it. Just go ahead with the brief conversations 'cause you will remember their name later and there ain't no sense in hurting someone's feelings. Besides you might even been kin to them and then you really would make a boo-boo.

All this might sound a little like you are a part of a cast with made-up lines, but that is not it at all. It's a way of life. People really care about each other. Sure, a name or two might not come to the top of your head quickly, but rather than hurt someone's feelings, go along with it. It's a warm feeling to talk to others in the bank line or post office, buying groceries or purchasing a deer call. It's nice to have acquaintances and friends in the places you frequent. Besides, everyone needs others, and I promise you a stranger or a friend will be there, if you need them. Small towns are like that, especially in the South. You are there for them and they are there for you.

# Paul Owens: A True Survivor

Paul is one of the most colorful characters in Galivants Ferry.

Ya'll know him but you don't know how he grew up. He grew up right behind my house. His grandma Callie and his granddaddy William raised him.

Paul "stayed on the hill" (which means on the banks of the Little Pee Dee River swamp). When I asked what he did most of his youth he told me, "I used to eat red clay – we thought it was candy." I also ate bark and bugs – my family thought I was gonna die –a local doctor thought I had TB and had 2 days to live...a farmer from the bay field took me to Florence to another doctor cause no one else could take me. Found out it was just worms from what I'd been eatin'."

He loved riding around with Son Daniels, who worked for Pee Dee Farms. Son drove the feed wagon pulled by mules. Paul would help Son feed all the multitudes of farm animals such as cows, mules, hogs, donkeys, and horses. Paul said he loved mostly "roaming the woods from one end to the other." He knows the land, swamps, rivers, bogs, timberland, farming fields; he's known it all his life. We call him the "outdoor executive" today.

Paul has always had a temper, but he can keep it under control most of the time. Not so in the past. Paul said "I'd cuss anybody out for a nickel," or "sing Jesus loves me for a dime."

His uncle Rufus had several stills. When Paul tried some, he said, "When I drank wine out of them barrels, all I saw was double vision." That still was located right behind our house – that's why we have so many wild grapes there. It was the still that made beer that "tasted like Pabst Blue Ribbon." The other still made moonshine – Rufus got put in the penitentiary for that one. Years later when he got out of prison, someone killed him at the Bloody Bucket, the only hang out in Galivants Ferry.

Paul loved his grandma, Callie. He told me, "Saturday was scrubbing day. I pumped two tubs of water for the ringer washing machine. One day my grandma had pretty white sheets hung out on the clothesline right beside a big mud puddle. I jumped in the mud and then wrapped myself up in them sheets – she cried big old tears – I felt so bad but she could all of sudden go on the warpath – she was part Cherokee. She was small but hell on wheels"

Paul grew up in the rough part of the Ferry, a part of which I wasn't aware, thank God. He said, "If you wanted to see a fight, just go any Saturday afternoon to the fillin' station." That's what we called the old Esso station. One time, he told me, "A man bit the nose off of another guy at the station and then that guy bit a hunk out of the butt cheek of the man. There was blood comin' out the corners of his mouth!"

Another story he recalled at the station was about another local man. "When he went to drinkin, he could be pissed off in a hurry. He whipped some little boy on the face and it left his handprint. The little boy went next door to the store, bought him a knife and gashed the fellow on his cheek. In fact, the man's tongue stuck out through the gash. I'm glad I didn't see things like this but it appears from listening to others this was normal. In fact the yellow Case knife was and is today considered to be the 'Horry County Special.' Horry County considers itself to be "The Independent Republic of Horry," so some things just happened and nobody told the police. People just went on 'bout their own business. They learned who not to mess with.

Paul has some "young and dumb" stories. "Once I told the preacher I wasn't gonna quit drinking 'til my toes curled up – I'd fight my shadow cause I was bad. I started going to jail every weekend cause I drank way too much. I asked God to take the taste away – it's been 21 years since I had a drink but I still love my cigarettes…Your granddaddy would have loved that comment."

Again, Paul really is an "outdoor executive." Your Daddy gave him business cards so he could hand them out. Learning what Paul knows today has taken him nearly all his life. He's always loved to hunt and fish and is one of the best in Horry County.

His most incredible skill is trapping. He started doing this in the 70s with steel traps. He had to use thick gloves to get his hands on the critters he would catch. Among the critters were possums, coons, beavers, bobcats, foxes and coyotes. These animals needed to be trapped because they ate all the baby quail, ducks and deer. Paul said, "I could sell coons for 2 or 3 dollars apiece." Beelie, his neighbor, loved to eat the possums. He said, "The other critters' pelts and hides could be sold, too."
Paul had and still has a passion for trapping. He started building his own traps out of sticks. "I'd eat anything I caught except possums."

As time went on, new methods of trapping appeared. He bought fox pee, gland lure, coon pee, coyote pee after the steel traps were outlawed and replaced by rubber traps. Paul had to learn new ways of trapping, which he did. He told me, "I'd bury the rubber trap, put wax paper over it, sift dirt on top, level it out, dig a bait hole behind the trap and put road kill as bait in the hole. Then I'd put a scent pole stick (which had the lure on it) next to the trap. The scent pole stick really *stank* and would last two whole weeks."

Paul ain't leaving the Ferry. Being raised here with seven other children (really his uncles and aunts) and his sister Thelma, his family roots are here. He still loves the land. If you ask him if he wants to go somewhere else, even to visit, he'll tell you, "No." He's been to a few other places but he says he doesn't need to go anywhere else. He's married to a wonderful woman, Glenda. He has three children. Guess what he named them?! From his first marriage he had his firstborn daughter, Paula, named after him. His second born was also a girl that he named Hunter, and third born was a little boy, named Fisher. Paul said that if he ever had another kid he would name him or her Trapper.

"Ain't no way!" says Glenda.

### 

"Paul, you're a true Survivor."

"I really am! I tell it like it is," said Paul.

"I stayed at Grandma's 'til the 60s. I was five or six when I moved to Marion, SC with my ma. She decided to raise me after all. I went to elementary school in Marion. I was in the first grade with Miss Denise Skipper. I went 'til the 7th grade but I left after two weeks of the seventh grade. My step daddy raised hell with me all the time. He grabbed me and I knocked him down. I never looked back and headed to Galivants Ferry. I walked from Marion to Galivants Ferry. I have been here since then.

"I stayed on the river for six months on "Joe Patch" on the Little Pee Dee River. Had a frame tent I got from the boy scouts. "I was happy to be in Galivants Ferry. Set up all night catching catfish, and then sold what I caught off the pole. I'd sell what I caught to WM, Teena, and who else wanted 'em. Uncle Rufus taught me how to fish traps. He was a great person. You just had to know him but not listen to everything you heard about him. He walked me through the swamp on his shoulders. I learned a lot from him. When I stayed on the river for six months when I was 13. I was not scared of nothing. I slept on the bank, under the moonlight, watched the stars. I'd like to go back there for a few days."

While Paul and I were talking, he saw I had a Dasani water bottle on the desk. He suddenly said, "I could catch all the fish I need with that bottle."
"Huh?"

"Yeah. Get the bottle and some nylon cord and a number three eagle claw hook, catch some bream, scale them, cut 'em up in little squares, put 'em on a hook and throw out the bottle. After a while you'll see the bottle bobbin' up and down. One night I caught 41 butterball catfish (swamp cat fish) like this. They are the best to eat!"

###

Fisher, Paul's son, is just like his daddy. He wants to do everything His daddy does, "I put him on the trapping permit so he can set his'n. He catches as quick as I can." Fisher tells Paul he's not only Daddy but also Best Friend. "I raised my kids good," said Paul.

"After I came out the river I went back and stayed with Grandma on the hill. I started raking leaves for the Holliday Brothers five and a half days a week. I worked with Rob Owens (bless his soul he died at age 93). Then on to the fillin' station, I worked there for two years and with Tommy in the store, I loved lifting fertilizer I had a 28' waist. I was tough, so I thought. I was 18 year old then."

"There were a right good number of women after me. I went back to the river for a while with one of them. I had a great time. I enjoyed 'bout everything I've done. There were a few moments not great but I came through. I got in a fight at "the joint" (aka: the bloody bucket) with a man he stabbed me with a pen. I almost lost a kidney. They took me to the hospital and they put me in a gown with no rear. I left there in that gown with the butt open. I got me a six-pack of beer and went home. I didn't give a rat's butt."

I asked, "How did you meet that 4-titted lady?" He said, "I was in the picture show in Marion. I met her there. When she took off that bra I figured it all out. She was a blessed woman, I know she was the first and last of women like that I've known. I stayed in Marion at that time. I was 14 and she was 13. Parent's back then didn't give a rat's butt."

"I got married in 1976 for the first time. I married Lou Ester Privette. I stayed married to Lou Esther for 13 years. She was 15 years older than me. "Friends to the end." I sat with her when she had emphysema. She was a good woman. I never had nuthin' bad to say about her. She had three younguns before we got married and we had one girl, Paula Jean. She lives in Texas with her husband Eddie and my three grandkids, Amber, Megan, and Colton."

Y'all, Paul's life stories could go on and on. Just when I think there are no more off the wall "Paul Tales" then I hear another one. All I can say is he is the most unique person I have ever met. If we had a *LOST* episode or an *Amazing Race* in the Ferry area he would win hands-down. Paul is a multi-faceted crystal. The more you see Paul and get to know him, the more you realize you do not know about him. One thing I know for sure is he is a loyal man, a good father, a good husband and my friend. I am privileged to know him and we got lots more years to learn 'bout each other.

When y'all come home be sure to spend time with this fine man. You will learn more about life if you sit down a spell and talk with him. Cross my heart and hope to die.

# Aretha

The sweetest lady in the world passed away. But away? What does that mean?

In this case, it means that without a doubt she is in heaven. She was one of the most loving people I have ever known. Her name was Aretha, also known as Reef, Reefie, Weef, Weefie, Reeth, Mama, and Reetha. My family and I had the honor of knowing Aretha for over 25 years. She helped me raise my children and inspired me to become a better mother and wife.

A harsh word was never uttered from her mouth. Thus the saying "if you don't have something nice to say about someone, don't say anything at all." 'Keep your mouth shut' became an example in real life of how to treat someone nicely. In other words she taught me to 'do unto others as you would have others do unto you.'

Aretha had a show-stopping smile and personality. The warmth of her being pervaded the whole room the moment she walked in. She made people happy. She never criticized others. Her words were like silver boxes wrapped in gold ribbons ushering in good will to all she met.

She was the best mama in the whole world, too. She had four children of her own. And I am blessed she took my three children under her wings. They loved her so much. We all loved her. We still do. I can feel her hugging my heart right now. It's the same tightness you feel when you're sad. I believe that is Aretha hugging us from Heaven. She doesn't want us to be mourning.

My favorite bible verse is John 14:2: *"In My Father's house are many mansions; if it were not so, I would have told you. I go to prepare a place for you."* It gives me comfort every time I read or recite it, because I can see Aretha in my mind. She's got a brand new body, and she's got a huge suite in Heaven with someone else taking care of her. Her smile is lighting up rooms in her new heavenly home.

While I was with Aretha in the hospital, after she had gone to Heaven, I noticed the screen of a machine above her head. It said: 'The patient has temporarily gone to the operating room.' Why hadn't I noticed this before? Perhaps it had been there all along. Truthfully, I feel it was a message from God. Aretha was temporarily on earth in this large operating space. But now, she has moved to her permanent abode with her Heavenly Father. We too will transition one day and by God's grace will see Aretha again.

I pray we can follow in Aretha's footsteps. It will be hard to do. She was and still is a "one of a kind" lady. With God's strength, I aim to try each day. One day she'll be waiting for us all, with open arms, and of course a huge smile on her face.

We love you so much, Weefie! See you soon. Keep the lights on.

# The Brightest, Most Colorful Funeral Ever

Recently, I attended a black funeral. It was the brightest, most colorful funeral in which I have ever been privileged to participate.

At first glance, the church hall was filled with people ready to pay homage to the deceased like at most funerals I have attended. As the procession began, I realized this was not going to be a "normal" funeral.

The preachers entered first one by one, followed by an army of Masonic brothers. Then came the family. They were all dressed to the nines. Distinctive distinguished men, women and children dressed in fitting attire of such materials as lace, taffeta, well-fitted suits and dresses, starched white shirts and pleated pants, polished shoes and appropriate patent leather heels or dressy flats depending on the wearer. There were attractive hats adorning many throughout the parishioners. The hats were adorned with feathers, lace, and other adornments, all very neatly worn. The Christian crosses worn by many were not worn just for "that" day. You could tell the crosses were a part of those wearing them – engrained in their souls.

This was not going to be a "farewell." Oh no, far from it. It was more of a "bon voyage," homecoming, or some sort of "life celebration" for the departed person. The excitement was building.

The choir was composed of all men. And boy, did they have the voices of Motown! Let me hear you say "Amen!" I felt like calling a talent agency. I just might do that. An American Idol, or two, is in residence at this country church. There was, however, a female soloist that could have been Aretha Franklin's backup or partner. She sang her heart out. Let me hear you say amen again!

The music filled the chapel, the people on their feet, their hands clapping in rhythm to the soulful choir and their bodies moving to the beat of the spiritual music being sung. There was a distinct feeling that there was a spirit moving amongst us, penetrating the atmosphere and filling in the gaps where most needed. It felt good.

After some wonderful hymns, a variety of speakers spoke their stories about the person who was in the grey shiny casket. Only the body was still there. They were talking to the family to give them comfort. Their stories were intuitive, soulful, joyous, and funny. They all reiterated how they had been blessed by having known the deceased. They shared out loud the many gifts that their loved one had left them. (Don't you think we should all share our love verbally before a passing occurs? We should remind each other to make a list of all we wish to tell others and how much we love them and what gifts they have given us.)

In the sanctuary, there were nurses in crisp white uniforms scattered about, keeping their eyes on their flock in the pews where they gathered on this special day. If one needed Kleenex to wipe a tear, the box was passed. If you needed a hug, there were open arms ready to hug you, even if you did not know each other. I liked the idea that being emotional and showing your emotions was so acceptable.

As the preachers gave their message, the church became even brighter. There was a spirit among us. Maybe there were angels in the sanctuary making us feel like we were "one." Two of the preachers appeared to have halo of lights behind their heads and upper bodices. I felt there were spirits joining us and soothing the attendees. If you have ever felt like you are all alone, experiencing moments like these will erase all thoughts that you are truly by yourself. That is comforting. Folks in the church who were strangers acted like they knew the person sitting next to them or standing among the crowd that gathered. All greeted each other with smiles, tears, hellos, goodbyes and "nice to meet you's." As in most Southern occasions, most wanted to know who your folks were and how you knew "so and so." There was a sense of "oneness" and "solidarity" for the two hours we were together.

How come we can't hold on to these feelings day to day?
As the family was comforted, others were encouraged to go hug on the family, right in the middle of the service! Sharing and showing your emotions at times like this is one healthy way to deal with difficult situations. I was grateful to be allowed to offer what solace I had and be comforted as well.
Truthfully, I received much more today than I can put into words. I was an outsider today to most in the church, yet I was made to feel so welcome and accepted. As a writer, the words to describe these interactions are hard to come by. The word, "warmth," comes to mind.

Forgive me for calling this a so-called "black funeral." It was anything but what the adjective infers. Black is only a color, and it was by far the most beautifully colored funeral I have ever, in my life, attended. All spectrums of the rainbow were pervasive during the service. The colors were passed from one to another and the emotional colors in the sanctuary were indescribable. I found myself reaching out to collect as many colors as I could. I left the church feeling fulfilled with many no name "new friends," it was a God thing. It was a special day.

I was supposed to go to this funeral. An hour before I was supposed to be at the church, I realized I did not know how to get there. I called the widow of the deceased and dialed the wrong number. The person who answered was one of the preachers for the funeral I was planning to attend. He stayed on the line and directed me to the church. Like I said, it was a god thing. It gives me goose bumps thinking about it.

Bottom line: We all come into this world in the same way. We all leave this world in the same way. We take nothing with us when we leave. As a friend's song title says, "the hearse ain't got no trailer hitch." We need to try and remember we are not promised tomorrow. We need to make the most of today. When we leave this world or when others leave they cannot take "stuff" with us but we can leave our gifts to others in the meanwhile before we meet again.

# The Murrow Family

I wish you three had grown up with a man like William Murrow. He could do anything.

He is one of the first people in Galivants Ferry that really stands out from my childhood. He was there every day taking care of our animals and working for my mother in the yard, while also keeping an eye on me. William mainly helped me with riding horses. He would have them bridled and saddled for me when I came home from school. When I was a very young girl, he would lead me around while I held on to the saddle horn. As I got older he would let me ride alone, but he made sure to close all the gates so if the horse ran away I couldn't go into the highway!

William protected me. I could count on him to be with me whether I was riding horses, driving go-carts, climbing trees, or skating. When I was outside playing, you could bet your bottom dollar he was within sight or ear range. If a horse took off, William could stop him. If I got thrown off, he'd be the first to pick me up or call for help. I was a tomboy, so cuts, bruises, and broken bones went with the territory. One special talent he had was the ability to "talk" warts off of the body. Ask Jane Graves: she will tell you.
Paul Owens described his grandfather; "He was a hard worker." He was born and died here at the Ferry.

William married Callie. They lived right behind our house and raised seven children plus two grandchildren. Their children were Donald (the baby), Michael (died in a car wreck), and Rufus (shot at the Bloody Bucket after serving time the penitentiary). He and my brother George were good friends, playing baseball in our front yard. They also had Carol Ann, Jean, Willie and Thomas (he died as a baby). They raised two of Jean's children, Paul Owens and Thelma. These two were my age, so we played together growing up. Thelma was smaller than me, so I loved passing my clothes down to her. That's what people do in the South. Waste not, want not – don't let anything go to waste!

Callie was a quiet, small lady. She was part Cherokee, so her skin was a little tanner than most. She was kind, sweet, loving and a really good ma, grandma, and wife. I will always remember her fondly. She took care of all the Murrow's and they held her in high esteem. She raised the kids with no TV, but they would go across the street to Joanne Jenrette's grandfathers, Dan's, to watch television.

You can't replace people like Callie or William. Paul Owens says of Callie, "She was sweet, I loved her to death, but when she got mad, she was hell on wheels."

I know nearly all Callie and William's younger ones and those that worked at the store, Pee Dee Farms, or at the Fillin' Station. Willie and his wife Cathleen were kind enough to let me talk to them and (pick their brains) for memories. They brought pictures for me and I've inserted them in this book because they were our neighbors for my whole life.

One morning in particular was about my brother George, your uncle you never met. Willie, who worked at the station at my father's request, changed George's tires. When Willie found out that George had been killed in a wreck he asked my father, "Mr. John was it my fault? Were the tires the problem?"

"Willie don't you worry, it had nothing to do with you or the tires," my Daddy told him.

That relieved Willie, but nothing was ever the same after the accident. He told me my Mama would not come out the house for a long time. My father was someone else. I was young and immature as a twelve year old that I didn't really see all of this. (Or I just didn't try to understand.) "Your daddy was a good man and your Mama was the sweetest lady," he said.

He wanted to know why I wasn't as sweet as Mama; he said no lady would ever be as nice as Mama. He said she always made sure the Murrow's had food. This made an impression on him and he will never forget how giving Miss Margie, my Mama and your grandmother, was to their family. Thank you, Willie, for that kind word. Men got most of the attention during those days. It's nice to hear such good things about my mother.

Paul asked me to add some more information about his Uncle Rufus. Rufus always played with your Uncle George. He and George were buddies. They shot pool together, played baseball, and were good friends. I wish they were still here. Things would be different for sure.

Rufus was like a father to Paul. He was his eyeball. When you tell stories about interesting folks, you tend to elaborate on certain events. In this case, we'd like to emphasize very clearly what a good fellow Rufus was to Paul.

I recently asked Paul what he wanted people to know about Rufus. Here is what he said.

"He was a fine fellar. He loved to fish, he loved to trap and he loved to hunt. He was good at it and he taught me everything I know. He always toted me out to the swamp and set me on stumps in the streams surrounded by water. I was little, maybe 4 or 5 years old. I'd hear all kinds of things. I'd hear owls, whippoorwills, and bob cats. Agh!! I was scared to death. Rufus would tell me "Son, you'll be all right. I'll be back in an hour or so. I got to check my traps. He'd leave me on a stump in the swamp so nothin' could get me."

I asked Paul why Rufus took him to the swamp at night when he was a youngster. "He was learnin' me the ropes about the swamp, the animals and their sounds. He was just like a Daddy, brother and friend. People had the wrong idea about him. If people say something bad about him, I would get shook. I caught my first fish with Uncle Rufus. It was a nine-pound mudfish. I jumped on its back and Rufus hollered for me to get off. He told me that fish would bite you like a bulldog. He's got razor blade teeth."

Paul said he understood what he meant later in life, the day he was bitten by a mudfish. "It hurt bad. He ate my thumb and almost took all the meat off the bone. Back then we would put kerosene on it and then put spider webs in the gash so it would heal up. Rufus protected me to the highest! Nobody messed with Teeny Boy. That was my nickname. Another thing Uncle Rufus taught me was if you killed something, you ate it. He even made me eat a sparrow that I killed. He'd tell me we wasted a life if you don't eat it.

"When it comes to me and Rufus, like most kin folk, blood is thicker than water."

This saying is definitely true in Galivants Ferry today. You don't talk bad about other people's kin lessen you're ready for a fight.

# 134: The People Who Lived in the Thicket

I recently took photographs of some old mailboxes in front of the big white fertilizer barn on Highway 501. The road that runs between this barn and the Big Red Barn used to be Main Street.

I guess you could say it still is. The many people who lived down this street were the glue to Galivants Ferry. There were other areas that I will discuss later, but this area is referred to as The Thicket. I remember as a child there were at least 12 homes in the Thicket. I imagine it was called the Thicket since there were many pine, oak and other trees surrounding these homes. They were made of white clapboard and had tin roofs. Some had front porches, while others had side or back porches. Chimneys topped all of these houses, which were full of happy families. The last house on the road was where your Granddaddy was born along with all his siblings.

Most of the houses are gone now. There are flowers that come up each season where they had been lovingly planted. You can tell where the houses were. I hate they were torn down. But at least five are still left! The mailboxes still have numbers on them and old red mail flags. "134," one mailbox reads in green handwriting. As luck would have it, the house still stands — with "134" handwritten on the door!

Now I am determined to find out who lived in all these houses...the ones still standing and the ones torn down.

I remember visiting with these folks when I was young. We would ride horses over to this area and visit on our way to the "bone yard" (the cemetery for farm animals). Also, Daddy would ride me around to speak to people and say hello. It was fun riding around and visiting neighbors.

Everyone who lived here, all the families who worked and built their lives around Galivants Ferry, are part of our history. We must remember not only our direct blood kin, but also those who were part of and an integral member of the township.

# Clyde Register: A Man of Few Words

Y'all never met anyone like Clyde.

I never met anyone else like him, either. He single handedly kept Galivants Ferry clean. He was the original "trash man," only he used mules and a large wagon instead of a garbage truck to pick up the trash. He never had much to say, but he didn't need to talk for you to know what he was thinking. He had a huge job, took it seriously and did it very well.

I can remember hearing the clickety-clop of the wagon wheels as he entered our driveway. He always wore a tan hat with a broad rim, overalls, a white shirt and boots along with a faint smile and curious eyes ... blue, as I recall. He was an honorable man, took care of his family, and lived in the red house next to the Big Red Barn during my childhood. One of his daughters, Linda Johnson, found this picture for me. She told me, "When Daddy said something, you had better listen, even if was just a 'yep'."

The Ferry would not have been complete without Clyde.

# Beelie and Martha

Clyde Register married Maggie Perritt.

Her mother was Martha Perritt, and she had a brother named Beelie. I don't remember the names of all their other siblings, but I do remember Martha and Beelie as if it were yesterday. They were colorful folks. What I remember the most was they lived in the thicket across the street from us, where Judson's house is today. Judson and I liked to run through the thick pine straw and make "lean to" tents out of new fallen straw in the thicket.

We loved to play in that area next to where Beelie and Martha had their wood-clap home. It was hidden from the road where the porch surrounded it. Judson and I would sneak up and listen to them on Saturdays. There were lots of liquor stills. I'm not sure, but I believe Martha and Beelie engaged in this moonshine.

Sometimes, Judson and I would sneak around them like kids to acting like we were cowboys or spies. We had our BB guns so we could shoot birds or just acts like we were hunting. If Beelie or Martha heard us, they would yell, "Who's bad out there?" Every once in a while, Martha would shoot her 12 gauge single barrel up in the air, and we would run away so fast. We knew they would not hurt us, but we still liked to act scared. Like now, you had to protect yourselves especially if you lived in the woods by yourselves.

Beelie and Martha were good people; I miss them. Since I was so much younger I was just a little kid to them. Beelie worked mostly with Judson's family and helped drives us around in a small green pony wagon. He protected Judson like William Murrow protected me. Again this is another example of extended families in Galivants Ferry. We all fit in the picture some way or another.

# The Davis Family

The Davis family has lived in Galivants Ferry for years and years.

WM (that's how he spelled his name) was the big daddy of the Davis family. He drove Daddy and Uncle Joe all over the place. It's a good thing speeding was common. WM got them wherever they were going safely. However, sometimes they would end up in the wrong city. One time, your granddaddy took a nap in the back seat of the car, and when he woke up, he was in Savannah. They should have been in Columbia. Daddy always had a good laugh about that.

WM was married to a lady named Eva; they had a mess of young'uns. Their names were Monroe, Jerome, Sammy Earl, Harvey, Willie, Henry Lee, JW, Leroy, Chris, Aretha, Letha Mae and Laura Ann. The two to which I've been closest are Henry Lee and JW. Y'all know JW; he is like a brother to our family. He has taken care of our animals and Mama's yard for a long time. Suffice to say, JW loves all our animals and us. We all love him, too. His brother, Henry Lee, worked in our yard for a while and had a green thumb.

One day, Henry didn't show up for work. I knew he had been sick. JW was worried about him, so he came and got me. He was scared to go and check on him. I told him I would go with him. When we got to the house, we could not get Henry to come to the door. We pushed the door open, and when I went in, I found him. I had to tell JW and his brother that he had passed away. I know God was with the family and me that day.

Henry Lee is gone but he will never be forgotten. He was a skinny, sweet man with a great big smile. He helped in many other ways, but this is how I remember him the best.

Families like the Davis' were always there for us. They took care of us and loved us and we did our best to take care of them. We were kin. We are kin. We will always be kin to the families of Galivants Ferry. It all goes back to the golden rule: "Do unto others as you would have them do unto you."

# The Peavy Family

I cannot reminisce about the Ferry without conjuring up memories of the Peavy family. They were and still are a huge family. I can't talk about all of them 'cause I don't know them all, but I do want to mention a few.

### Charlie Peavy

I loved this man and he loved me. How do I know? I just knew. He was the father of Aaron Peavy and others. I reckon you'd say he was the head of the "Peavy clan." If it weren't for the Peavy family I really don't think our family or the community would have thrived like it did. Charlie was a small-framed man who always had a smile to share and he told the truth. Even if you didn't want to hear it.

### LB Peavy

What a wonderful person! He treated me like I was one of his children. He took me to school, picked me up and carried me to special occasions. Even though his real job was running the Esso station as you came into town, he also played a big part in my school years, 'cause Daddy and Uncle Joe wanted him to take Judson and me to wherever we were supposed to be going.

He wore an Esso cap on his baldhead and drove Daddy's Cadillac, which made him look a chauffeur. He'd park right outside the school windows and people would say, "Christy your chauffeur is here!" That drove me crazy. He just would not take that cap off. I was embarrassed, but LB was proud to pick me up because I was like his own daughter. He has a fish on his gravestone at Galivants Baptist Church.

### Billy Peavy

Billy had thick black curly hair. He worked around the Ferry, too. He was a little younger than the other ones who drove us to school. Sometimes he drove us to school and I'll never forget how fast he drove on those back roads to Mullins! It was a race every morning down Pee Dee Road to 917 and on to McCormick Elementary School. The bell jumped on us and rang as we ran in the front doors and dashed down the halls to homeroom. Made me feel like I was in a NASCAR event! It was worth being tardy. Thrilling.

## Aaron Peavy

Aaron was one of Charlie's children. He's a handsome Christian gentleman, married to Kathleen, a beautiful woman inside and out. Aaron and Kathleen faithfully attend Galivants Ferry Church, and when I return there, they still give me big 'ol hugs!! I love them. I met them at their house not too long ago and found out Aaron had been a Navy Seal. He doesn't talk about it. He doesn't want to brag.

He also told me something else I didn't know. Aaron also drove me here, there and yonder and was told to protect me, Aunt Russell and Uncle George. He said "Mr. Holliday told me to protect and keep an eye on us because he was afraid of kidnappers."

To sum it up, the Peavys were kinfolk. They were a part of my life nearly every day at the Ferry. Even when I went off to boarding school and college, one of them helped take me there and got me settled in. Special, fond memories surround my images of them.

# The Store Folks

Okay, I want to again emphasize that I considered everyone who farmed with us, worked in the Esso fillin' station, tended the farm animals, managed our timber, or worked in the store or post office to be kinfolk. Blood ties put you in the same family tree, but love and acceptance would extend your Ferry family. It still does. Here are some of the people I grew up around at the store.

### Tommy Doyle
My first memories of Tommy draw back to when the store was a true country store. Tommy was in charge of the meat department. We had a true butcher shop. The fresh cut bologna was my favorite, and the scraps Tommy saved for me were the "cat's meow" for all our animals. As time went on, Tommy took charge of the whole store. There was something for everyone. The store carried not only groceries, but also clothes, boots, farm equipment and family necessities. You didn't have to go to Aynor for anything. Tommy had it all. We had a really nice bond and worked together when we "modernized" the store. We should have left it alone.

### Marvin Skipper
Marvin was an integral part of the store when I was little. He was the manager at one time. Marvin was the best fisherman in the area too. He took me fishing in the lakes at Mary Long's and showed me how to catch redbreast and bream among many other swimming critters. Once, a snake fell in the boat with us!! I 'bout had a heart attack. Those memories of fishin' with Marvin are still fresh in my mind. My daddy did not fish, so I'm glad Marvin took me.

### Bill Davis (Daddy's Shadow)
If y'all mention Bill Davis' name anywhere among the education or farming system in South Carolina, you will get something like, "Sure, I knew Bill. He was a wonderful man." Bill worked hand in hand with your granddaddy John Monroe and your Great Uncle Joseph Holliday. I have his office now that he's gone. It was a sad day when he passed away. Mr. Bill had grounded common sense. He was a pleasure to be around and kind to all. He was like a brother to Daddy and your Uncle Joseph and another father figure to me. He loved meetings, tobacco and the Farm Bureau.

## Ed Richardson and Emory Graham

I combine these two because they worked together like two peas in a pod. They double-handedly took care of details with our farmers, farms, buildings, houses and miscellaneous details. Ed always smiled and wore a hat. He was truly a handy man. Give him a hammer and nails and Presto! He'd fixed whatever was broken. Emory was little quieter but also amiable. He didn't talk a lot but he had impeccable manners. "Yes ser, that's alright, uh huh" were common to his conversations. He made sure things got done. He and Ed reported to Mr. Bill, Daddy, and Uncle Joseph. I liked to ride around with them.

## Elise and Cecil Dix

These two occupied the post office and office ever since I can remember. Elise did everything in the office. Primarily, she was a secretary, but she also worked in the post office and eventually became the first woman postmaster of Galivants Ferry. I remember her being in Daddy's office taking "dictation." Daddy sent out memos all the time, and there was no computer back then, so the dictation procedure was the way Daddy got his memos out to people. Elise was and still is a very pretty lady. She was always dressed up with not a hair out of place. Her husband, Cecil, was a mail carrier.

# Donnie Christenbury

A beach legend died recently.

Donnie Christenbury was the king of pool parlors and shag dancing. He was also a people lover. Russell knew him very well, but I didn't know him as much, since I was a few years younger, However, I knew him well enough to know he was the 'Real Deal.' He represented, to me, the epitome of a classic figure from the good ol' southern beach areas and in particular the Grand Strand areas of Cherry Grove and Ocean Drive. He represented the beach culture many remember and cherish.

Donnie reached out to everyone, including me. (Even though I was underage for being in beach joints). Back then, in the 60s, the cops were not so strict, and if you weren't drinking, you were okay. In addition, legal age back then for everything was 18. Donnie was a legend in his own time, a master at both shagging and shooting pool.

The first time I met him was in his own pool parlor at Cherry Grove. It was called DONNIE'S. Russell would take me there on summer afternoons to play pool. Donnie had given her a personalized pool stick. It screwed together, had her name on it and even had a leather case. She looked like a pool shark. The two of us were a sister team. Russell would ask other players (always males) if they would like to play a match of 8 Ball with us. Of course the men did not take us seriously. Most thought they would give us a chance. After all, my sister had long blonde hair, deep tan, blue eyes – and her partner was her little sister. What did they have to lose? Russell taught me not to be afraid of competing against men. You just did not beat men at anything back then... it was not proper for a southern woman.

We cleaned their clocks most of the time. I don't remember the statistics. Donnie watched us out of the corners of his eyes and tried not to laugh out loud when the Holliday sisters were in action. I guess you could say he is responsible for these wonderful memories. It was his place, his pool tables, and he welcomed us.

The beach will not be the same without Donnie. His big smile and sparkling eyes were like a magnet. He was a good soul. Donnie made everyone feel at home around him and we will miss him.

# Denise Skipper

Denise was the glue that held Holliday Associates together. Without her, I am not sure what we will do.

Y'all knew Denise extremely well. She was a Godly woman, honest and fair, as the day is long. She was also like a sister to me. We've been through lots of drama together and she always could keep her cool. Like I said, she was the glue and the balancing tool, similar to a "leveler," which every complicated family business needs.

I asked her what was one of the reasons she stayed for 25 years. She said, "Mr. John made history exciting." Daddy, Bill Brown, and Bill Davis hired her at the time both Holliday Families shared the offices at the store.

During the interview she told me that Daddy had warned her, "Young lady, if you ever drink from the water of the Little Pee Dee River you'll never want to leave!" "I never did," Denise told me. She added with a giggle, "I stayed, but I bet we've been through at least 25 secretaries since I started."

Denise and your grandfather got very close over the years. She told me, "Mr. John trusted me. He valued my opinions. He knew I'd check on him, and I did." She went on to say that through the years "he depended on me," and "he trusted me." "Trust is one the most important things between people. You can't trust just anybody." She was asked to be present when our families flipped a coin to split the family properties. She attends any important meeting. She kept us calm. Like I said, she was the glue.

One of the funniest antidotes she told me about your grandfather was his love of telephones. "Mr. John told me he'd have to put a phone in the casket before he went to the 'wild blue yonder.' He always said he'd keep a phone close by so he could call Miss Denise." Then she told me a titillating story having to do with Daddy's phone in his office. "Ever since Mr. John died, his phone in his office was turned off. One day several years ago the phone started ringing in his office! I went to pick it up and no one answered. Somehow I just knew it was Mr. John calling to check up on me." I, too, believe it was Daddy. He probably knew Denise was sick and wanted to comfort her. He knew she would know it was him.

I asked Denise how she could work with our crazy family for 25 years. She told me she loved working in a family business. Every day she learned something new and different. I promise she could run our office blindfolded and single handedly. I don't know what we'll do when she's not here.

During a brief interview for this story, I asked Denise to describe some of the employees she knew well, just a phrase off the top of her head to describe them. Here is what she said. She loved working with most of the employees of the past 25 years. Some are still here; some passed on to work elsewhere, and some have actually passed away:

"Matt Lynn, our CPA before Johnny, worked as hard as he could. He was a nice man."

"Mr. Bill Davis loved to go to meetings of all sorts. He was a wonderful man. He had a big heart, presented himself well, plus he represented the family in a good light."

"Mr. John never met a stranger. All who visited the office was asked to sit down, have a small Coke and a pack of Nabs."

"Tommy Doyle: he defended the underdog."

"Paul Owens: I loved him but he was a scoundrel; he straightened himself up, thank goodness."

"Post office workers Elise Dix, Marilyn Roberts, Jinx Best and Cecil Dix kept the old post office alive 'til it was moved to Aynor. That move upset all of us."

Denise's take on growing tobacco; "I don't think tobacco kills as many as they say. I never smoked. My Mama has smoked since she was 15 years old. She's 75 now."

She told me how Johnny, her husband, came to work at the Ferry. He took Matt Lynn's place. At the time Denise was asked to work at the Douglas Company too but she stayed at the Ferry cause it was home. Most people don't understand how Johnny and I worked together. It worked well."

Paul Owens added a funny anecdote to this story. It shows how much fun Denise is. She and Glenda played a joke on him. They gave him a phone number to call. They told him he had won a box of fishing equipment from Tidewater, a fishing store, and all he had to do was call a number to get his box. He called and asked for his box and a man said, "I don't believe you need a box yet Mr. Owens." He was the undertaker. They all got a kick out of that prank.

It's hard to fathom that I interviewed Denise only a few weeks ago and now she has passed on to "the wild blue yonder." She braved cancer for too many years and now she is in her new outfit in a better place. I wish I had written down more from Denise, but we thought we had forever. You know, we are not guaranteed tomorrow, so we better make hay while the sun shines.

Denise was such a multi-faceted woman. When I think about her, I see all the colors of the rainbow. She reflected the goodness around her. She defended the truth and called things like she saw them. She had a talent of setting things straight very diplomatically so no one's feelings got hurt or got angry. She just knew "the truth be known" which is another way of setting the record right. She had a great listening ear and knew how to keep what she heard to herself. No doubt, she spoke her mind and did not mince words but she knew how to do it or when to be quiet. She set a Godly example of a southern woman.

We all miss her. The office isn't as bright as it was when she was there. She would not want any of us to grieve for her. Her faith was so strong that she even wrote a letter for others to help them. That's how she was…always helping others. I would like to share one sentence of her thoughts she wrote down:

"Jesus can save you. He can heal you in this life but sometimes God wants you to be with Him."

I bet y'all she has some sort of phone with her right now so she can locate Granddaddy and all her family and friends. I hear heaven has a big house and I am sure she will be able to find everyone quickly. She always was very efficient. I wouldn't be surprised if she is a heavenly manager. I wouldn't be surprised if she found a way to call and tell us she is doing well.

# Josephine and Marvin Skipper

*"If it hadn't been for them Hollidays..."*
*"They deserved everything they had..."*
*"There were resentments but they were so good to us..."*
*"Your grandfather took care of us..."*

It was so nice to hear these kind words from Josephine Skipper.

She and her husband Marvin have lived in Galivants Ferry forever! They were the pillars of the Galivants Ferry Baptist Church while I was growing up. They are still a vital part of the Ferry fabric that holds the past and present together. They know lots of stuff.

Marvin was hired to be the manager of our Pee Dee Farms general store in 1947, where he stayed for 14 years. He had many stories; I'll tell you a few. He told me in the old store there was a cooler for meats. With the help of Press Daniels, Carl Peavy and Clyde Register, Marvin would kill the cows from the farm in the big red barn. He said they would hand 'em up to him and put them on a big meat block so Marvin could 'cut 'em up!

Every Saturday morning was meat cuttin' day. The farmers would come to the store with their wagons to buy all sorts of items. Fatback was a nickel a pound, hoop cheese was popular and all necessary grocery items was available to go along with fresh cut meats. The store even sold clothes! Lingerie, boots, jeans, shoes, fabrics and sewing necessities were all for sale. The store catered to the farmers, so there were barrels of seeds, fertilizer, nails, and screws. You name it! It was a one-stop shop for the folks at the Ferry. If y'all want to, we can go explore the old attic and you'll still see remnants of this historic store. Our family really never throws anything away, and now I know where we got this notion.

Marvin wanted me to tell y'all your granddaddy "was a wiz 'n business." He also said your Uncle Joseph, Judson's daddy, "was a shrewd business man." That sounds like a good combination, doesn't it?

# The Bayfield Families

Y'all are very familiar with the Bayfield, but not its history.

I've interviewed lots of folks to get their impressions of this gem of an area. To me, it's part of the heart of Galivants Ferry. This area not only was home to many fine families over the past 100-plus years, but it's also one of my dearest memories.

Let me tell you why we call it the "Bayfield." Certain low-lying areas near the coast are considered bay areas. Way back when, it was legal to ditch the area to keep the land dry for planting crops. As a result, the soil was great for a variety of crops that were grown here like tobacco, soybeans, family gardens and pine trees. It was and still is a very fertile area. The central location made it perfect for families. They were close to the store, the Big Red Barn and the river. They could hunt and fish easily, plus they were walking distance to the Galivants Ferry Baptist Church. The Bayfield was a good central location for everything needed at the time.

The families who lived in the Bayfield were sharecroppers. That basically means we owned the land, they lived in our houses and we split the profit after all debts were paid. That's a very simplified definition of sharecropping. They helped us and we helped them. I've enclosed a letter for you to read from one of our farmers, Mr. Daniels. I was glad to read it because some people say sharecropping was not so great. Since we don't farm like this anymore, receiving letters like the one that follows this piece is very nice.

For the most part, farmers had their own area to grow tobacco. It was consider "King", because it was a cash crop. I've described in another story how grueling it was to grow tobacco, so I won't go through that again. Just know all tobacco farmers worked extremely hard. Like all farming, some years were good and others were bad due to too much rain or not enough rain, plus disease and pests. The farmers also had corn to make, their own wheat, sugar cane to make sugar products, and cows to produce milk and other dairy items. Different farmers had different animals, and they all had their own vegetable gardens.

It was never easy, but the good Lord took care of them. Daddy used to always say, "God takes care of farmers, Democrats and Baptists."

There were many other farmers scattered all over Horry County, but the farmers who lived in the Bayfield were our neighbors, since they were across the street. Daddy would take me driving with him to visit them. Sometimes I even got to ride a horse across the highway to the dirt roads that connected these farms.

I remember happy faces, lots of children and kind words in the Bayfield. In many ways, I was jealous of them. They had so many people to play with and lots of family. The highway between our house and the Bayfield was almost like a barrier of some sort. Or maybe it was just in my mind.

Every several years, there seemed to be a turnover in the houses in this community. New folks would move in, so there were too many farmers to name who lived in this heart of the Ferry. Because I was so young, I cannot remember all the families that lived in these houses. What was engrained in my soul was these people were kinfolk. Even though I personally don't remember all their names, the warmth that permeates my soul when I visited them has left a lasting impression.

If I had three wishes, they would be to restore the old homes, move the families back in and y'all to meet them. I reckon for the meantime, until I get magic powers, y'all will have to take my word for it. When you read the letter from Bobby B. Daniels, you will see what I mean.

In the beginning, tobacco farmers only farmed about two acres. As farming modernized, they could handle more. This trend led to fewer farmers but larger farms. When this transition happened, the Bayfield turned partly into a dove field.

# Part IV
## The Historic District of Galivants Ferry

# The Galivants Ferry Stump

I told you this wasn't a history book, but I'm going to tell you about The Stump because the history of it is important.

Wade Hampton, former Confederate General and Chief of Confederate General Robert E. Lee's Cavalry Corps, began his campaign for Governor of South Carolina in Horry County when he spoke to Horry County Democrats at Galivants Ferry, South Carolina on September 30, 1876. This marked the beginning of Democratic dominance in South Carolina politics for the next 100 years. The occasion set the precedent for the Democratic primary speakings that began soon after and continued to be held every two years on the banks of the Little Pee Dee River at Galivants Ferry. The site was named for a man surnamed Galivant, or according to a 1820 map, "Gallwant." A ferry was operated at this site to carry people across the Little Pee Dee River.

Joseph W. Holliday, a naval stores and turpentine entrepreneur, operated a time-supply mercantile business at Galivants Ferry, which served as a community gathering place. His store became the site for political leaders to speak to voters. In those days office seekers would address the crowd by standing above it on makeshift platforms such as wagon beds or heavy boxes to be heard. Local legend has it that the use of the word "stump" to describe partisan oratory evolved in earlier times when people may have literally stood on tree stumps to be above the crowd. The Galivants Ferry Stump Meeting evolved as a biennial event that brought politicians and their supporters from across the state to the banks of the Little Pee Dee River. Today in Galivants Ferry, the wagons and boxes have been replaced with stages, sound systems, flags, news media, banner planes and audiences numbering up to 5,000.

In the beginning, there were 12 to 15 primary speaking engagements, or stumps, throughout Horry County. The Galivants Ferry gathering was always first on the circuit. The last stump meeting took place at the county seat in Conway on the Saturday before Election Day.

The Galivants Ferry Stump Meeting was held in a pine thicket across from the general store and continued every two years during the lifetime of Joseph W. Holliday.

When Joseph Holliday died in 1904, his son, George J. Holliday, inherited the mercantile operation and with fellow Democrats, he organized a local Galivants Ferry Democrats Club that continued the tradition by moving the site to the rear-loading platform of his general store. The event continued every other year. George J. Holliday's term as a State Senator from 1903 to 1908 allowed him and the stump meeting to rise in political stature. From 1936 to 1942, Press Daniels, president of the Democratic Club – or Executive Committeeman as known today – was very active in organizing the event.

After the death of George J. Holliday in 1941, his elder son Joseph W. Holliday followed in the tradition of his father and grandfather by promoting stump speaking from behind the scenes. Like his grandfather and father before him, he served as Postmaster and officially could not participate in partisan politics. He was helped by fellow Democrats Bill Davis and Marvin Skipper. Meanwhile his brother, John Monroe Johnson Holliday, the youngest son, was at The Citadel preparing for a distinguished career in the U.S. Army. After World War II and an extended term of service, John Monroe Holliday returned to Galivants Ferry in 1945 and soon became both front man and principal organizer of the event.

Today, Joseph and John Monroe's families continue as hosts for the Galivants Ferry Stump Meeting. John Monroe Holliday was proud to preside over the first Galivants Ferry Stump of the new millennium held on May 1, 2000. Unfortunately he died four months later, but his daughters Russell Holliday and yours truly are continuing his efforts. Joseph's heirs, Billy Holliday, Judson Holliday and Betty Holliday McLeod are equally involved in planning this historic event.

In the late 1960s, many other stump meetings began to fade as TV, radio and expanded newspaper coverage brought more immediate political news into America's homes. John Monroe Holliday fought relentlessly to keep the Galivants Ferry Stump Meeting a state tradition. Through his tireless efforts, the Galivants Ferry event continued to grow in importance to state and local politics as other stump meeting disappeared. It gained such importance to state and local politics as other stump meetings disappeared. It gained such importance, that many believed absence from the stump to be a "kiss of death" for any statewide Democratic Candidate.

When stump meetings first began, all the politicians attending were primarily Democrats, since there were few Republicans in the South. Naturally, since it was a Democratic event, only Democrats spoke. Although it is still a Democratic event today, the event holds such importance and draws so many people, that as many Republicans as Democrats attend. Nevertheless, only Democrats are invited to speak

The Galivants Ferry Stump Meeting is also where the legendary U.S. Senator Strom Thurmond debated and beat ten candidates for Governor in 1946. He then became a Dixiecrat, and years later, a Republican. It was also here in front of this family-owned general store, where U.S. Senator Fritz Hollings began his long political career as a candidate for state Lieutenant Governor in 1954. He did not miss a stump meeting for the next half-century.

Some of the other famous people that have started at Galivants Ferry are Governor Cole L. Blease, Governor Pitchfork Ben Tillman, Senator Cotton Ed Smith, Senator Olin D. Johnston, Senator Burnet Maybank, U.S. Secretary of Education Dick Riley, Governor Bob McNair, Ambassador John West, U.S. Ambassador to the Court of St. James, Phil Lader, and Secretary of State under President Harry Truman, Jimmy Byrnes.

Some might also remember Senator H. Kemper Cooke, the backwoods statesman who ran for Governor. One of the most memorable was Dero Cooke who played his Stradivarius violin at the Galivants Ferry Stump and then announced his candidacy for the Presidency of the United States.

Statewide recognition of the political importance of the Galivants Ferry Stump Meeting has grown. This is evidenced and enhanced by increased statewide and national media coverage. In 1986 was featured on NBC's *Today* show and, in 1990, on ABC's *Good Morning America.*

To make sure that the 1992 Presidential Campaign was an integral part of the stump meeting, the Governor Bill Clinton and U.S. Senator Al Gore sent Congressman David McCurdy of Oklahoma to represent the Clinton/Gore ticket. Congressman McCurdy had been one of the people who nominated Bill Clinton for President at the National Democratic Convention in New York.

What makes this event unique is not only that it has endured so long, but also that it has grown in recognition and importance in an age where TV, radio and newspapers have generally taken the place of old-fashioned in-the-crowd politicking. There were once many stump meetings throughout the South, but the Galivants Ferry Stump Meeting is the only one that has retained its appeal and viability. This event draws many people from across the state to a place called Galivants Ferry that has no industry or main street-only a combination general store and gas station. There are no schools and no stoplights...but the people come.

This historic event is usually held on the first or second Monday in May. It begins at 4:30 PM with old-fashioned clogging and country and gospel music by the Red White Family with Billy Holliday often joining them. Chicken bog, South Carolina's version of jambalaya, is served by the local chapter of Masons or the Lions Club from the neighboring town of Aynor. The official ceremony begins at 6:00 PM, with the opening remarks made by the ranking Democrat present. The speeches, music and chicken bog continue into the evening.

It has been said that the Galivants Ferry Stump Meeting is a slice of pure Americana and an example of Democracy in its original form. This is now recognized by the Library of Congress, which has selected the Galivants Ferry Stump Speaking as part of their Local Legacy exhibition.

My very first memories of the Stump come from the 1950s when Fritz Hollings was running for Governor. His logo was "It's Fritz." I wore an apron with this printed on it and went through the crowds giving out stickers, buttons and fans. That's when Fritz named me, "Little Monroe."

Other memories include my daddy, Uncle Joseph and Bill Davis introducing the political speeches, limiting the number of minutes they could stand on the podium and talk. If you didn't limit them we would be there all night.

Some of the past politicians, I remembered besides Fritz, are Joe Riley, Joe Biden, John Spratt, and James Clyburn and Donna Christensen. Of course there were many more, but I mostly enjoyed watching the festivities and visiting with friends.

Some of the extras were Red White and his String Band, cloggers, chicken bog, the pilot club's cake sales, and the TV reporters with all the lights and cameras. The Stump was and still is a big deal! It's the last and oldest in the world, run continuously by the same family for 134 years.

In 1990, *Good Morning America* came to interview Daddy. To my surprise, they also interviewed Aunt Russell and me. I'll never forget Bryant Gumbel say "yuck" on National TV when they described chicken bog. He's obviously not a Southern culinary expert!

All the men that ran this event for years have all passed away. Now it's run entirely by women! We found out in a hurry this was not an easy thing to do. Not only do the politicians change every two years, all the contacts change as well. Plus, we had to computerize everything and add some more "color" to continue to attract the crowds.

Because of the modernism of our times, there are too many choices where to spend your time. We wanted to make sure we could continue this tradition and still attract the crowds. After all, as Daddy would say, "the Stump would give you the chance to talk eyeball to eyeball" with your future leaders. You can't do that watching TV. Daddy said many times, "The Galivants Ferry Stump is Pure Americana." It is a family tradition. But most of all, it is pure, clean fun!

### 

Here is an example of why the Holliday Family continues this tradition. This was featured in *The Sun News* in 2010 before The Stump, and it was written by your Aunt Russell and me.

*The Sun News*
*Letter to the Editor: Written 2010*

*The Galivants Ferry Stump Speaking is more than politics. Yes, we want it to get good coverage all over the state in the political pages because some people only read that page. We do not say that this is only for Democrats. Everyone is invited.*

*A lot of people come to The Stump although South Carolina has not voted presidentially for a Democrat since Jimmy Carter. However, the fact that Joe Biden, a middle of the road type person, Democrat, has picked Galivants Ferry, a town with no stop light over many other invitations is amazing. This is a man who delivered the Eulogy at Republican Strom Thurmond's funeral and is best friends with Democrat Senator Fritz Hollings. C-span will be here for their series, "Road to the White House," which will air on May 7th. What is going on? Is this a turning point? You have to admit it is a very interesting point.*

*What we are emphasizing is that all parties are invited: Democrats, Republicans, Independents, Undecided and Frustrated…Of course, only Democrats are allowed to speak because we honor 134 years of tradition. What makes this interesting to EVERYONE is we have created a festival type atmosphere to interest those people who aren't excited about "political events." We decided to make it colorful, fun, with things to do, entertainment, southern food (chicken bog), funnel cakes, "stump water," buggy rides, donkeys to pet, people dressed up handing out hats, flyers, bumper stickers…National Shag winners, cloggers, cast members from the play, "1776," performing songs. This will bring people in and at the same time offer them a free arena to be able to hear, meet and speak with candidates. To look at them "eyeball to eyeball" as our father would say. People yearn for the time when a handshake was the same as a contract.*

*For the history buffs, we emphasize that five generations from the same family are putting on this event in the same area where it all started 134 years ago!!! And now it is all women! In 1876, women couldn't vote! We are amazed that our father did what he did with his brother Joe and it looked easy but it is not!!!! It's about to kill us and we are half the age they were! See our web site and see the flier announcing the Galivants Ferry Stump in 1876… It was a governor's race where General Wade Hampton came through on horseback and spoke to a crowd in Galivants Ferry. (His win started 100 years of Democratic Governors in South Carolina.) Now 134 years later, we have 3 gubernatorial candidates speaking at the same place in 2006!*

*The ultimate thing we would like to get across is that we have to get people motivated to vote, to think...We are a democracy. It is a privilege to vote and it is your duty to get informed and to vote what you think, not what your friends or your parents tell you to think. If 18-year-olds can defend our country, they need to vote. All ages and social strata need to know that their opinion does count and that they CAN make a difference! They need to ignore labels like Conservative and Liberal. What is liberal to some is not liberal to others. What is considered conservative for some is not conservative for others. People just need to be open-minded and to think.*

*A lot of people who think they are Republican but are asked their feelings and thoughts on some issues, may be surprised to find they think the same as many Democrats. Many people who think they are Democrats have some thoughts and opinions that are the same as their Republican friends. Labels need to be ignored! What do you think? What does your candidate think? Choose based on that not on whether or not they are a Democrat or a Republican. There is a blend! Hopefully, we can find a blend that is best for this country. Maybe we could go forward if we were each open-minded enough to listen and think for ourselves, not what we think our friends or family want us to think!*

*We hope we can provide this historical event in the historical district of Galivants Ferry to get more people to think. Maybe if we can get more people here for non-political reasons.... for the festival and food, we can get them more interested in our country and more motivated to participate in the political process. By osmosis, they will become more politically aware and active. This is what we try to provide through the Galivants Ferry Stump Speaking.*

*Hope to see you on Monday, May 1.*
*The Holliday Family, Galivants Ferry*

### ###

The 2010 Stump was a wonderful event chocked full of personalities, entertainment, friends gathering, and politicians talking.

Thanks to our good friend Fritz Hollings, this event can be found as a Local Legacy in the Library of Congress. If it's Gods will, and as Poppa would say, "If the Little Pee Dee River don't flood," y'all as part of the fifth generation are next in line to hold the reigns of this small piece of history.

Have fun with this; add your own flavor to our Historical Holliday Legacy. The Stump celebrated its 134th year this past May. Keep it going with your cousins and your grandfather would tell you maintain this "slice of Pure Americana."

And now, a little culinary delicacy symbolizing the Galivants Ferry Stump...Chicken Bog.

## Galivants Ferry Stump Chicken Bog

- *2 ½ lbs. of cut up chicken*
- *1 lb. smoked sausage*
- *1 large onion chopped*
- *1 tbs. Worcestershire sauce*
- *2 cups of long grain white rice*
- *4 (or more) cups of the broth produced when you cook the chicken*
- *Salt to taste*
- *Pepper to taste*

*Cook chicken in large pot in water with onions. Cook 'til done. Debone and set aside the chicken, then cut into pieces.*

*In the same broth, cook up bite-size pieces of sausage 'til done. Set aside sausage with the chicken. Measure 4 cups of the broth (or a little more). Bring the four cups of broth to boil in another large pot or the same one reserving the extra broth in case you need it. Add the 2 cups of rice. After 10 minutes, add chicken and sausage to the rice, and simmer 'til done.*

*This will serve a family of five. Of course, it can be multiplied for mass quantities. Enjoy this classic Southern meal. It goes well with rolls, string beans, slaw, sliced apples, and of course sweet ice tea.*

# The Galivants Ferry Church

The Galivants Ferry Church lies nestled under oak tress dressed in grey, Southern moss.

It will always be a simple homey church...the church where I was raised. Inside, the clear large window panes let in all the natural light and give you a good view of a small part of God's world outside.

I never knew just how much this little country church meant to me until recently. Investigating my memories, digging deep, this simple church not only influenced my life but it helped shape the soul of the Galivants Ferry Township. The church was critical to the Ferry's society, structure, stability and survival.

Your Great Granddaddy Joseph William Holliday gave the site and building materials for the church in 1885. His second wife, Mary Elizabeth Grissette was its organizer. According to the obituary on your Great Granddaddy, "He (your great grandfather) was a Christian but not a member" and never attended this church (taken from his obituary). It is an interesting point but right now I want to tell y'all what I recall dearly about my church.

Attending Sunday school and church every week was a given. It's what you did without discussion. I remember my Daddy having to light the pot-bellied stove ahead of time so the large one-room sanctuary would be warm by church time. The seats were old "picture show" seats. Nothing was wasted back then. I am not sure, but I bet they came from one of our old movie theatres we used to own.

Sunday school was held prior to church in one of two small rooms behind the sanctuary. There weren't many children, but we received good lessons from the teachers. The hymns *Jesus Loves Me, Come into My Heart Lord Jesus*, and the prayer, "Now I Lay Me Down To Sleep," are some of my first ingrained memories of going to church.

During the preachin', everyone stayed to listen...even all the babies and the older people clearing their throats. There were lots of crying and other background noises, but no one seemed to mind. We mostly heard from traveling preachers. They came when they could, maybe every other week. Sometimes, a preacher would preach several Sundays in a row, which was a treat to the congregation.

Marvin Skipper started the service most of the time when I was little. My Aunt Frances Holliday taught the adults and Daddy taught the younger adults. I recall Daddy studying the lesson in the den at home in his brown leather recliner. You did not bother him when he was studying his Sunday school lesson. Shirley King played the piano. She did her best...sometimes she would miss notes, but we just kept on singing and it worked out since not many could carry a tune. Sounded good to me.

As I got older, we actually had some regular preachers like Rev. Gordon Graham. That was special, but eventually the regular preachers went on to a bigger church. We understood but missed them. We sang from the Broadman Hymnal. It remains my favorite hymnal today because it has all the traditional Baptist songs I grew up with.

The music from the Galivants Ferry Church still echoes in my head. This is one of the ways I realized what an impact this church had on me as a child. Today, out of the blue, I find myself humming tunes and singing words from these old hymns. The words and tunes comfort me and bring me back to balance. It's hard to explain, but when things get topsy-turvy, and feelings of sadness surround me, or I am just confused as to what to do about something, 'they' just pop in my head…and there's no pushing them out 'til 'they've' had 'their' say.

I have to list the hymns that float in and out of my soul…Here they come: *Just As I Am, What A Friend We Have In Jesus, Onward Christian Soldiers, Amazing Grace, Blest Be the Tie That Binds, Holy Holy Holy, I Surrender All, Rock of Ages, Shall We Gather At The River, Take Time To Be Holy, Trust and Obey, Nothing But The Blood Of Jesus,* and *Love Lifted Me.*

I do not know all the words to these hymns, but parts of each song and certain phrases are imbedded in my heart. Thank God.

Lots of folks attended the Galivants Ferry Church. I remember the faces but not all the names. Since I am working from memory, I want to tell you who seemed to be there all the time. Some of these people I have covered in the "colorful characters" part of my letters to y'all. For now, since we are talking about the church, I want to rattle off the names of some…. Marvin and Josephine Skipper plus many other Skipper families, Purdee Parker and his whole family, all the Perritts, the Peavys, the Richardson's, my Uncle Joe and Aunt Frances' family, the Daniels, the Collins, the Murrows, and the Brooks families.

There were many more, and they all did their part to build the Galivants Ferry Baptist Church's family. There was an invisible bond between everyone. We were all different, yet the same.

Christmas programs were very popular. Santa Claus came to visit, the real tree shined with colored lights and icicles, and mountains of presents piled under the tree for all. Everyone got presents, even if they had never attended services there before. Everyone also received lots of oranges and apples — and even candy on some years!

Your granddaddy loved knocking on the back door to find Santa…He would bring Santa in and all the children would start clapping and smiling. The happiness warmed up the church even more. On this night, attendance was standing room-only. All were welcome and love pervaded the atmosphere. Of course, we sang hymns like *Oh Little Town of Bethlehem,* and the Christmas story was read honoring the birth of Jesus.

Another strong memory of mine was when the preacher would ask people to come up at the end of his sermon. When this happened, we always sung *Just As I Am*. This was the chance for anyone to come up and accept Jesus as their savior. Some Sunday's people would come up...then again on many Sundays nobody would come up. I felt sorry for the preacher when no one came up to the altar. After all, he had tried his best...maybe next Sunday.

If you came forward, your next step was baptism in the Little Pee Dee River. You aren't christened when you are a baby in the Baptist Church. Some might baptize infants or toddlers today, but not when I was little. We would gather at the banks of the river behind the Ferry store. I remember my sister Russell being doused in the black water of the river. The preacher held onto her head, gently leaned her backwards and placed her whole body and head in the water.

By the time I came forward, things were different. I was taken to some strange church with a huge tank of clear water, and an unknown preacher baptized me. To this day I want to be baptized in the river. Someday, I will be.

Not long ago I went to the Galivants Ferry church all by myself. I mentioned Daddy always wanted me to play, *What a Friend We Have in Jesus,* on the piano in the church. I did. I know Daddy was there with me as I played. It felt good fulfilling this age long promise.

# The Big Red Barn

Y'all can't pass by Galivants Ferry without noticing the Big Red Barn.

That is, of course, unless you are driving blindfolded or speeding on the way to the surf 'n sand of Myrtle Beach. Actually, I think some vacationers speed up when they get to the Ferry and see the Big Red Barn. It means they are getting closer to their final vacation destination.

The Big Red Barn is an icon of Horry County on Highway 501, and one of the largest old barns in the United States still standing. Way back when, it was used for many activities including raising cattle, mules, storage of tobacco and general storage of farm equipment. I remember these uses because, for Judson Holliday and me, the Big Red Barn was our personal playground.

In 1928, Press Daniels built the barn out of the thickest widest boards you have ever seen. It has three floors, an elevator and large entrances with ramps big enough to drive mule-drawn wagons or tractors all the way up to the second floor. While growing up, I did not appreciate the actual usage of the barn. I *did* appreciate the large floors with alcoves and storage areas to play hide and seek in. It was always kinda dark in the barn, which made playing in it even more fun, because this added an air of mystery. If you played in the barn, you had to either be a male or a tomboy. I was the latter.

I remember Judson and I used to try and crawl on the cows or chase the mules or just explore like we weren't supposed to be there. Scavenging through the old relics of years past always entranced me, and jumping in the corncribs was a great way to get filthy dirty. If you didn't get really dirty, that meant you were not playing hard enough. I liked getting dirty, even though most of the time this meant I had new scabby knees or arms. I liked playing in this wonderful barn almost as much as climbing the big magnolia tress in my yard or riding horses to the bone yard.

Next time y'all come home, let's go play in the Big Red Barn. It still stands as a monument to the South I knew and to a once thriving farming community. I feel a resurgence coming!

# Jack's Lookout Road

B.R. and Patsy Gaskin took a drive with me not long ago and described Jack's Lookout Road and how it got its name.

It's a half-mile from us, and it's one of the last dirt roads around here. BR.'s daddy & kinfolk owned this land. They farmed it and they had a country store where all who were hungry were fed every day. Like others of that time, they had chicken coops, cows, tobacco, and their own vegetable gardens. On this road sit barns that were once some of the most beautiful I've ever seen, but they're in bad condition now. It's hard to watch them decay, so y'all better enjoy them before they fall down!

I asked B.R. & Patsy how this road got its name. The story I was blessed to hear, with a deep Southern drawl, goes kind of like this.

### ###

"Well, you see, in my father's and grandfather's years, times were hard. This road wasn't even here yet. It was over there. That was when there were only wagons and mules. There's a slough of the swamp over there and you had to go through mud to go anywhere. Right 'round the corner, there was a church. 'Cause we had colored folks workin' the farm, they needed a church. It was built right there. See how there ain't no trees? That's where they had their church."

"Like I said, times were hard. People were rough. The Ku Klux Klan had a lot of power, and lynchin' was common. In order for the preacher, whose name was Jack, to watch out for his flock, he'd open all the wood-plank windows. You know, the kind with hinges. That way, he could see outside so he could 'look out' for his congregation in case someone from the Klan was tryin' to sneak up on them. That's why they call this road Jack's Lookout Road."

# Sharecroppin' Pecans

First of all, it's pronounced pe'-can...not pecan.

Now what is sharecropping? My family has sharecropped many kinds of crops in years past and we still do "share" the pecans. This simply means whoever wants to pick up pecans around our yard (friend or stranger) follows one rule and the gathering begins. The one rule is you take half and I take half. You shake hands and the deal is sealed.

This arrangement helps everyone. I love to sit in piles of pecans and leaves and look for these prized nuts but that takes lots of time. Picking them up as you lean over can produce a prize backache. So, sharing your pecans is good for all.

At the end of the season we all have plenty of nuts for baking and sharing with friends. Here is one of your grandmother's favorite recipes.

## Marjorie Russell Holliday's Cheese Biscuits Topped with Pecans
- *1 lb butter (room temperature)*
- *1 lb sharp cheese (room temperature)*
- *5 cups plain flour*
- *Sprinkle a dab of red pepper (about a quarter teaspoon)*
- *Salt (just a dash)*
- *Pecan halves*

*Grate the cheese and cream with the butter. Cream thoroughly. This is not as easy as it sounds. I use an old timey mix master. You can even use your hands. Gradually add the flour (little by little).*

*Now divide the dough into balls. You then make each ball into a long roll. This is best done on a clean counter. If it gets too sticky sprinkle a little flour over the dough to make it easier to handle. Wrap each roll with wax paper and chill (or freeze for later use).*

*Preheat oven to between 300 and 350 degrees. Get a roll of dough, place on counter and slice and put on baking sheet. Put one-half pecan on each slice. Bake until the biscuits are a golden brown. Do not overcook. Keep an eye on them as all ovens are different and you might like them less cooked than others.*

*Take biscuits from oven and let cool. They are now ready to be munched on, served as an appetizer or put in holiday gift boxes for special friends.*

## Margy's Toasted Pecans

- *1 bowl of clean halved pecans*
- *1 pound of butter*
- *salt and pepper*

*Preheat oven to 325 F. Place pecans on a large baking pan. Spread them out so they are not on top of one another. Dot with butter, cooking slowly light on. Keep an eye on them.*

*Turn them over several times 'til the whole pecan half is a crispy brown. Not to brown or you'll burn them. Sprinkle with salt and pepper as desired. Rest on a paper bag 'til cool.*

*Great gifts! Place in small tins or cellophane bags!*

# Goin' to the Beach

One needs a beach dictionary or atlas to list all the beaches in South Carolina.

Starting from the North end there is Tilghman Point, Tilghman Beach, Cherry Grove, Ocean Drive, Wendy Hill, Atlantic Beach, Briarcliffe and then Myrtle Beach. Heading South, you will run into Surfside, Garden City, Murrells Inlet, Litchfield, Pawleys Island, Debordieu, Georgetown, McClellanville, and then the Charleston Beaches. This area is known as the Grand Strand.

Some don't include Charleston, but to me, that's not very nice, so I want to mention Isle of Palms and Sullivan's Island. I guess you have to draw a line in the sand since you have Folly Beach, Edisto, and more going into Hilton Head Island.

It appears that South Carolina is a good ole beach state. Its wide beautiful strands hold gorgeous sunrises and sunsets, creeks, sand dunes, beautiful shells and warm waters for thousands of vacationers annually, not to mention the residents and old timers who have been living on these jeweled beaches for years.

The beach memories I want to bring to the surface are the ones I remember as a youngster, becoming a teenager and spreading her wings. Boy, we had some times to remember! I might need some help on this one. So many good times to recall.

"Under the Boardwalk...Down by the Sea" echoes in my head my first visit to the iconic Beach Club. It was located on Highway 17 on the north end of Myrtle Beach. That night was the first of many. The Tams were playing in the high ceilinged, beer stained floor and smoky building. I was about 14 and I was dating John Gandy, a good-looking, curly blond haired guy, and a great friend. It was so exciting to be in this famous building with a date, the band playing our favorite beach music, people shagging, singing and just hanging out. The memories are filled with happy people, youth bursting out, lively conversations and joyous tunes surrounding everyone and everything this building. It was like the Beach Club was isolated from the world. Perfect and classic.

The Beach Club was owned by the Corbets, an influential family, especially in the music industry. They were able to attract all the top performers in the beach music crowd and lots of big names from the Top Ten music scene. I will always remember George, my brother, inviting members of the bands to come to our beach house. It wasn't far from the Beach Club and George was so likable he could attract just about anyone to our home.

One time Major Lance came and sang his song "um um um um um…um um um um um…" as he walked around the pool table. George's roommate at Wofford College, Pickle, told me not too long ago that there were lots of exciting memories with regards to band members coming to play pool and hang out at our beach house. I wish the Beach Club was still there to showcase groups like The Four Tops, Smoky Robinson and the Miracles, The Entertainers, The Temptations, Drifters, Jerry Butler, The Fifth Dimensions, The Spinners, Peaches and Herb and many, many more. We had good clean fun shagging and enjoying the beach culture back then. Those were the days, not to be duplicated ever again.

But, I bet if the Beach Club was still there, y'all could get the bands to come visit the beach house again. It's a magnet of sorts. I'd bet money on it.

Another hot area of entertainment I want to tell y'all about is O.D., also known as Ocean Drive. O.D. had joints like Fat Harold's and The Pad that were also shagging meccas and still are today. The names change but the dance stays the same. I am not a good shagger by any means, but your Daddy and I do our best. I never got some of the moves down pat like the "belly roll." You three have certainly been around these areas growing up and probably have stories to tell about shagging that I don't know about. I kept secrets about my escapades at the beach from my parents. That is normal, but now I want to spill my beans about this era of my life before I forget any more details! If I tell will y'all tell?

We used to have house parties in Ocean Drive and Cherry Grove. They were wild times in those days with buddies from Mullins and Ashley Hall School. A little Budweiser, Hopping Gator, Boones Farm Strawberry Wine, and a constant lookout for cute boys, especially ones who could shag, were priorities.

Spring Break was the most popular time, just like it was when y'all were in high school and college. Renting a house with lots of bedrooms, finding a "chaperone", finding a bed without sand, and getting as little sleep as possible were the criteria for what we called 'having a good time'. The traffic would be bumper to bumper. Hitching rides with strangers was common. We would get so tired we would have to take time off from having fun, go to my family beach house in Myrtle Beach in order to get some sleep in a clean bed and eat Mama's vegetable soup. After a couple of hours of sleep, a hot shower and a meal, we were back to the party scene. My friends had to take turns going home with me to get rested up. See, we aren't so different after all.

There were many more places to spend your times at the beach, but there was nothing like getting a suntan. We had no idea what SPF or skin cancer was. Baby oil was the best choice for greasing your body down. All we knew was you had to "turn before you burn," according to the radio stations! If you weren't on a sandy towel on the beach, you were surfing or surf fishing. In the afternoons, a little putt-putt was perfect right before you went out to eat a fried seafood platter.

Then, it was time to visit the Pavilions. There were two that I remember. The biggest one in Myrtle Beach, the second one in Ocean Drive and a few smaller ones scattered around the smaller beach areas. You could ride roller coasters, tilt-a-whirls, Ferris wheels, merry go-rounds and a ton more. And they only cost so many tickets per ride. What a deal! Of course, the interior arcades and bingo parlors were a must in order to win really cool prizes! The haunted houses were actually scary and the bumper cars were always challenging.

The outdoor had arcades, too, like throwing darts at balloons and tossing rings over the tops of bottles. They always made me spend every dime I had 'til I got a treasured soft animal. It was always so rewarding walking out of the park with a squishy prize. Y'all got to experience a lot of these adventures when you were younger but unfortunately they are mostly all gone. It is so sad not to have a Pavilion in Myrtle Beach. I wonder if the rest of them are gone from the Grand Strand? I guess I will have to go find out, as this reminiscing makes me yearn for those old days. Since the old pavilions are gone, it might be time for me to have a rebirth of my shagging days. I just got to help keep part of the old beach era alive!

What else did we do at the beach? I already told you about sneaking out with Aunt Russell. Did I tell you about sneaking up on lovers in the sand dunes? Judson and I used to quietly ease up on young couples hiding in the sandy dunes. We never saw anything, 'cause we always got caught and had to run away.

Oh yeah, I almost forgot to mention skiing at Garden City Inlet and at Wacca Watche on the Waccamaw River. Waterskiing in the ocean or on black water was always an adventure due to large boats passing by with huge wakes or strange looking water creatures on the river. It was always just as much fun to stay dry and set up on a sandy spot like Sandy Island with lots of food, libations, and anything you needed for a day on the water.

It was also a big deal driving the boat to the famous Bucksport restaurant to eat a fine fried seafood platter. The last time I ate at this waterside café, we wrecked the boat in the cypress trees going around the curve. Along for the ride was Connie Cameron, Mac Carroll, plus a few more. We survived with a couple of broken bones and me with a broken nose, but we were tough and all was well. That might have been the last trip for me to Bucksport, but it sure was not the end of our skiing/boat days.

I used to frequently visit the Nichols, the Camerons and the Campbells. They all had family homes in Garden City with skiing boats anchored at their docks. They knew where to have fun in the sun and water. We also loved to go crabbing around the pluff mud creeks. A good old blue crab in a net meant good picking later for supper. A big basketful made a scrumptious feast. Ain't nothing better than fresh picked crabs…a southern delicacy.

As we got older, a beach trip would never be complete without a round of golf. Y'all know you were born into a golfing family and the beaches are covered with golf courses. I played more when I was young. That was a great activity for young people with clinics everywhere – plus, being a girl golfer provided a neat way to meet boys. Later, I played golf with all Mamas' friends at the Dunes Club. I was even runner up one year in the Dunes Club championship. I keep threatening to start playing golf again. It is in my blood. Reckon I will if I ever finish these recollections!

The South is blessed to have pretty beaches and South Carolina is extra blessed to have the Grand Strand. Y'all are lucky to have such close access to the beach. Whether walking, jogging, surfing and swimming, fishing, dancing, playing golf, etc…or getting into a little mischief, you just can't get tired of the beach. Thinking about and ruminating about growing up in the summer times at the beach has gotten my blood stirring.

Let's all go spend a whole month together at the beach this year! After all, we still got the beach house. We would be snug as five bugs in a rug (plus extended new family). I am excited! Aren't y'all?

# PART V
## My Life

# Normal is Only a Setting on a Washing Machine

Dear Holly, Russell and David Jr.,

I always thought I was normal. Russell, you sent me a card once and it had a picture of a housewife living in the 1950s with a dress and apron on, washing clothes. When you opened up the card, it said "Normal Is Only a Setting on the Washing Machine." That made me feel better because I do not think I have ever been "normal." Thank goodness I never wanted to be normal, and I still don't.

By researching this book, I've seen firsthand how people "categorize" one another. Some people assume all members of the Holliday family are spoiled rich brats. For this reason, I am determined to show that we all came into this world the same way and it is important to treat people as equals. You cannot assume you know how others feel or how they were raised. Money does not buy happiness. We are all God's children. With God's help, I'd like to break this stereotype. It's lonely being ostracized. The Hollidays are no different than any other large family.

This has been the biggest hurdle in my life. People judge and look at you different if they think you have money. I have already told you all that I never felt rich. Yes, I was fortunate, blessed and loved. I had friends, a very close family and was raised with good principles. I do not need to go in to this anymore. It does not matter what others think about you. It's how you treat others and how you think about yourself. Those with more need to give more. Not in money but in time, love, and giving of yourself. If money is a way to give, then that's good, but it's not the only way to give back.

When I lived here as a child, I was looked at as the rich kid, but, with my mother and father's upbringing, I was able to overcome this and fit in. We had parties that the whole class was invited to. My best friends knew me and thank goodness supported me and thought I was like them, I was. Why is it if you live in a big house in the country with some land do people consider you rich? It hurts me to this day. The friends I grew up with knew me, but now I have brought you all home...to my home...not where you were born, and I wanted everyone to accept you as the local, average kid. But in most cases that did not happen, and I am so sorry. I guess you have to prove it yourself and you all did for the most part.

I thought bringing you home, *to the country*, to Galivants Ferry, would encourage you to love your roots. You had learned to love your dad's Douglas family roots in Greenville. And then we tried to transplant you in Galivants Ferry. Not easy. Not an even path.

Holly was the first to go through some difficult times. I tried to take control and everything I did was wrong. After several years, she learned to love me again and I realized I was not in control. Then, Russell had her struggles with growing up. It was a rough row to hoe, but we made it. And you, David, Jr., it's your turn to deal with what-could-have-been. I know you will be all right and I will always be there for you. You know that. We are family. Your daddy and I love you all so much and we have done our best even though we could have done better.

I pray that y'all will find peace and happiness and look back on the time you lived in Galivants Ferry. Y'all have friends from many places. Y'all were born and raised in South Carolina. This is your home today. If you move like David Jr. and come back it will still be your home. I want you all to feel good in your own skins…I want you to feel good about who you are and where you came from and remember to always be good to others.

Life is not easy. It is a test, day to day. Sometimes good, sometimes bad. It is imperative for you to know that God has given you the strength to do what you need to do every day. If you cannot handle it, then all you are doing is too much, so let something go. I will always be here for you. Just call my name and even if you do not see me I will be there.

# Growin' Up in Galivants Ferry:
# From Kindergarten to Converse

I was born on October 18, 1954 right after Hurricane Hazel devastated the South Carolina coast. It also wiped out the family beach house in Ocean Drive just north of Myrtle Beach.

I have pictures of your grandmama pregnant with me, walking over the ruins of this home I, of course, never saw. A few days later, I was born in Florence, South Carolina They almost named me Hazel, which would have fine with me. I guess they thought better and named me Christian Monroe Holliday, the youngest member of the fourth generation of Hollidays to live in Galivants Ferry or elsewhere. I was named after a long lost relative named Christian on the Holliday side of the family and my Daddy whose second name was Monroe, his nick name. I reckon since they were going to name me Hazel that influenced God, and I do have hazel-colored eyes.

I came after a big storm and that might have something to do why I was, from day one, a headstrong Southern girl (or else I inherited a gene or two from my forefathers).

Thinking way back, the first vague hazy memory I have was having a birthday party with my immediate family and our cousins next door: Billy, Judson, and Betty Holliday, the children of Joseph and Frances Holliday. It was outside, next to the big white swing and the red swing set and red sliding board. My cake was a doll inside of a white buttery cake with rich yummy icing made to look like the big skirt of the doll. It's still the best cake I have ever had. Some more memories (maybe due to seeing the pictures I still have) include playing at the little playhouse behind what we call the Big Play House and next to the grape vines and dog yard. It's the one y'all played in when you were young. Judson and I had the best time making mud pies, mixing them with grass and trying to make people eat them. We also loved to dig holes to China and climb all the magnolia trees we could. Judson is the reason I was and still am a tomboy.

My first educational years were spent at McCormick Elementary School on Sandy Bluff Highway in Mullins, about 15 minutes away from home depending on who was driving the car. I want to summarize each year with the highlights for y'all so you won't put this letter down like you ignore my phone calls sometimes today 'cause you know I can be long winded.

### ###

**Kindergarten:** My first actual memory was in Kindergarten. At four, I was the youngest in my class. The first day at the Presbyterian Church in Mullins, we were asked to color a picture. I was so proud of myself and thought I had done the best job. I called the teacher to look at this beautifully colored page and to my dismay she said, "That's good Christy, but next time be sure to color inside the lines." *What!* I thought to myself. I guess that was the first time I showed I wasn't "normal." Who wants to stay inside the lines?

My second memory was being in the Christmas play at this Kindergarten. I was an angel with frizzy short blonde hair due to a recent permanent with a halo, wings, and a white fluffy outfit. I will show you a picture of me at this special event if you promise not to give your children a perm 'til they are at least old enough to agree. I think Mamas gave their little girls perms so they wouldn't have to brush their hair before they went to school.

**First Grade:** My teacher was Mrs. Collins, a jovial, sweet, white-haired lady who went out of her way to make you feel comfortable. The first day of school I got homesick and I think she let me go home. I loved first grade after that and met my first boyfriend, Bubba Hodges. He held me down at recess and gave me my first kiss. I loved it even though I said I did not. He gave me a friendship ring and I still have it!

**Second Grade:** My teacher was Mrs. Brown and I liked her, too. She was tall with brown hair, and I sat in the second row The seats were the hard wooden ones with a place to put your pencil, storage for your books and usually had chewing gum stuck under the desk along with etched messages in the wood from prior years.

I was Miss Second Grade and Daddy bought me a red dress from the Miami Airport for me to wear in the pageant. I still had really short frizzy blond hair. I was not the beauty queen and probably came in close to last.

My first lesson about being honest was in this classroom. I cheated for the first and last time in my life. It was a spelling test and the word was "have." I had a tiny piece of paper in my lap and I know Mrs. Brown knew it. I have never felt so guilty and I still feel my chest knot up thinking about it. I think I was trying to color inside the lines.

**Third Grade:** My teacher was Mrs. Shelley. She reminded me of Olive Oil, the girlfriend of Popeye (the sailor man cartoon character who ate spinach out of the can to make him super strong and he always rescued Olive. At the ending of each show, he always sang "I yam what I yam and I like who I yam, I'm Popeye the Sailor Man.") Mrs. Shelley was really tall and thin and had long limbs, like Olive Oil.

She always seemed to have a smile 'til one day during recess she told us President Kennedy had been killed. I was at a water fountain, the old cement kind that someone had to hold you up to when you were too short to reach it and the water never come up high enough for you to get water but you kept trying and you knew you were getting everyone's germs. I think Jane Graves and Susan Smith were with me. We were scared and school let out early.

**Fourth Grade:** My teacher was Mrs. Edwards, a pretty woman with thick brown hair and full red lips. The only thing I remember about this classroom is that I won "the child with the best posture" award and I got to stand first in line for lunch in the cafeteria. I was really proud of this for some reason.

Another thing I remember was my Mama and daddy took me on a trip all by myself and I got out of school for a whole week! We drove to Virginia and boarded the S.S. Rotterdam, a ship from the Holland American Cruise Lines, and departed in a snowstorm for a week in the Caribbean. It was rough. Mama was sick as a dog 'til we got below Florida, where the waves were so rough a big window broke in the dining room. I remember Daddy writing post cards home telling everyone Mama was horizontal for most of the trip.

It was the kind of trip where you had to dress up for suppers and had assigned seats in the dining room. I remember the waiters assigned to us to this day. It was such a special trip being with my parents by myself. On deck I was a hit, 'cause there were very few children and I won the limbo contest.

On costume night, Daddy and I dressed up as poor farmers in croaker sacks with poster board signs hanging around our neck saying "I made mine by farming." I remember riding a donkey with a floral lei in St. Thomas, visiting Blackbeard's castle in Barbados and going to a real bull fight in Caracas, Venezuela, where one of the matadors got gored and they actually killed the bull, the image of that day remain sharp in my memory. I never want to go to a bullfight again. It was awful seeing the red capes fooling that poor bull and then the final blow with the long daggers…No wonder so many matadors get hurt. I can feel my eyebrows crunch up thinking about it nearly 50 years later.

**Fifth Grade:** This is the year we had two teachers and changed classes. I hope I do not hurt their feelings, but I cannot remember the teachers' names. It might have something to do with the beginning of puberty and I had my eyes on boys as well as studying. Girl scouts were important, and Shorty McMillan was our scout leader along with Mrs. Burnham. I also loved taking piano lessons and kept my bike at Jane Graves' house so I could walk to her house and ride my bike to my lessons. I practically lived with Jane.

That was also the year I was thrown from my horse, Omen. I dislocated my elbow but that did not stop me riding horses. I don't think I ever told you three that right where our home is today was the location of a riding area complete with jumps. I rode western the first part of my life and switched to English. Genie Nisson from Marion came over and we had a teacher come and teach us. We were even in a horse show in Mullins. Daddy put up a fence with gates plus the white brick fence, and the gates closed around our home when we saddled up. It was critical for our safety so a horse couldn't take off towards the highway. We had William, our long-time yard man, close all exits to make sure anyone who got on a horse was safe. He took care of me. This pasture also doubled as a golf range. The whole family practiced here and then used our front yard as a golf course with trees and camellia bushes as the holes. We did lots together.

**Sixth Grade:** This was the first year I really had to study. The Student Council got my attention and running for office was fun. You actually campaigned and printed out cards, put up posters and made speeches. I won an office; I think it was vice president. (Slowly I was coloring inside the lines.)

This was also the year hormones poured in as well. Everyone had boy- and girlfriends. We traded around like mad. Spin the bottle, a game called choo-choo, and other kissing games became popular! I think y'all call it hooking up? We called it first base, second base, and third base. I promise I only got to first base. No kidding! A few of the boyfriends who were always in the middle were Bubba, Frierson, Wade, Randy, and John, just to name a few.

We also danced together at ballroom lessons taught by our teacher Mr. Turbeville. We literally had a ball learning all kinds of dances. My favorites were the shag, the South Carolina state dance, the polka, the cha-cha, and the box step slow dancing. Frierson was the star of the polka.

**Seventh Grade**: Now we had four teachers. Changing classes was something to really get used to, but we were the head honchos at the school. Mrs. Slaughter was the main teacher I remember, and she was tough. This is where I learned there was a world outside of Galivants Ferry and Mullins. She taught us geography and we traveled all over the world in our minds. We made scrapbooks about places like Persia before it became Iran and Iraq. USSR was there instead of countries like the Ukraine and Russia today. Germany was divided into East and West with the Iron Curtain. Yugoslavia and many other countries existed with different names and lines on the globe. What a different world it is today! I need to show you all the scrapbooks I made in the 60s so you can see how the world has changed!

This was an age of awareness for me. People started talking – about me. My friends didn't as far as I knew, but people who didn't know me just associated me with the Hollidays in Galivants Ferry, and they didn't want to give me a chance to be me.

I will never forget my parents would send L.B. Peavy, who worked for my family at the Esso station at the Ferry, to pick me up in their Cadillac. He was always early and parked right outside my homeroom class waiting on me. He wore a hat from the fillin' station mainly because he was almost bald, but he looked like a chauffeur and people loved to tease me saying, "Christy, your chauffeur is here!" I hated it. That was the first time I was embarrassed to live in a big white house in Galivants Ferry. Why were they making fun of me? Life as I know it continues.

**Eighth Grade:** This period of time was like the dawning of Aquarius. It was 1967. I was so sheltered from the world. No one talked about Vietnam. Where was this "Vietnam" country anyway and what did it have to do with me, us, Galivants Ferry, or Mullins? We really were sheltered from any true details of real life. Little did I know, I was getting ready to enter the most "real" days of my life so far.

This was the year we became true adolescents. Hormones were high, no one could hurt us, no one meant to hurt us if it happened, and everything would be ok. We were sub-freshman. There was no middle school yet...only high schools and we took over the eighth grade. Humph!

It was September of 1967, and such a wonderful period of time between the fifties and the seventies. Partying was in; Shag dancing was the rage for our part of the world, along with the beach scenes of Myrtle Beach. I entered the eighth grade arm in arm with my best friends in the whole wide world. We could do anything and we were scared of nothing.

Being the youngest at MHS had its plusses. We saw no negatives. We were in with the in crowd in Mullins High School. That was all that mattered. First you had to get used to this big old school with six grades all mixed up! That meant you were around all ages including the kings and queens of the sports like football and basketball. Being on a team made you cool. Being a cheerleader made you feel cool even if you weren't. Somehow I became a JV cheerleader. I was not cool but it felt cool enough for me. I did have a crush on the captain of the boys' basketball team.

To make what happened on the timeline clear to all of you, you need to know where my sister and brother lived at the time and what their lives were like. Russell was at Converse College as a freshman and she was the Kappa Sigma darling for George's fraternity. Uncle George was a senior at Wofford, pinned to the love of his life, Marion Sagar. Life as we knew it was great. Then the world we knew came to an end.

My brother, your uncle, was killed with three friends in a car wreck coming back from a trip to see the first snowflake of the year at Mt. Mitchell. The funeral was held outside in our front yard in Galivants Ferry. The landscape of people that filled the whole yard was overwhelming. There were murmurs like "how could God have taken such a fine young man away?" The line of cars from home to the cold cemetery in Marion was unending.

I remember thinking "this is not happening. This is a dream." People were staring at me. People felt sorry for all of the family. This was not happening to us. No, this was meant for someone else's family. We were the Hollidays and we were born with silver spoons in our mouths. What in the hell did that mean now! So much for fairy tale lives. George was buried, my sister went back to school, Mama fell apart, Daddy managed in his own manners, and I was left to raise myself.

Thank God the 'Ferry Families' were looking after me, and the other Hollidays were across the street plus Twin Graves, the mother of my best friend Jane, had her eye on me. Not to mention all my friends in Mullins. My support group included Harriett, Susan, Lucy Anne, Mary, Bubba Freirson and John. Plus many, many more.

I survived the eighth grade by the Grace of God trying to act like nothing was wrong with me. I lived, one breath at a time. Somehow, the fact this tragedy occurred, it made me more "normal" than anyone and my buddies.

**Ninth Grade**: In ninth grade, it was a lot of the same. I kept pretending all was well. You know how they say suppressing feelings is unhealthy? Well, I agree now but at the time I had high school to jump into with hormones raging, the beach calling me and a tall good-looking basketball player to keep an eye on. We all had licenses to drive cars and we were on the road constantly. Looking back now I think I was running from the past and hoping against all odds my brother really wasn't gone. I submersed myself in school activities, staying with friends, spending time at the beach and edging into blurry edges of adolescence. I was thirteen years old and ready to dive head first into teen years. So what if the Holliday name had ended with George's untimely death. Right now there was some serious fun to be had for us.

**Ashley Hall**: Either my parents wanted me to leave home due to the circumstances or this was in the cards the whole time. I was off to boarding school in Charleston, South Carolina, aka: The Holy City. I loved it from day one. It was a time of fresh beginnings, and boy I sure did need it then.

I had a great friend start with me. Mary Simpson, a school mate and lifelong buddy and I entered Ashley Hall at the same time. Driving up to this antebellum historic mansion would make most think they were at Tara in Gone with the Wind. Winding stairwells, large halls leading to hidden alcoves where hidden small dormitory rooms were placed, ballrooms, parlors, and hidden back stairs with wonderful older women ready to be our housemothers. One we called Pitty Pat. There was one for each hall and they lived in the same building with us like a real, live mother would.

When you lived in a place like Ashley Hall you made fast friends quickly. You became a big family along with all the good and some of the bad. My first roommate did not care for me and I don't blame her. I smoked a cigarette in her closet. I did not having smoking permission so I hid in her closet. I really did not mean to make her clothes stink of smoke. So much for making a friend with my first roommate. It was a bad thing to do but because of that incident I got to move in with my friend Mary. We were in the hall called Hay Loft. It was a good accident 'cause I met some of my dearest friends.

Here were a few: Nancy who had just returned from Africa and had tsetse fly bites all over her. Sylvia who wore her hair like pebbles the cartoon figure. Menard with a voice like a canary. Betty and Lura who shared a room from whence most fun began. I wish Anne, May, and others from that sophomore year could have been on the same floor but we were all like peas in a pod. So where you actually had a room of your own did not matter much.

Since you were not allowed much freedom we learned to improvise. Our outings consisted of one trip to the Red and White on Wednesday and a stroll downtown for a mandatory church attendance. That was not enough activity for us so at night we taught each other how to do stuff like French kiss using old big hair rollers. We also learned to pierce each other ears. These activities were done after 'lights out'. It never failed we would have one of the housemothers checking up on us. We would quickly retreat to our own rooms and sometimes we got caught, sometimes we didn't. In order to prevent these 'near catches' Lura, Betty, Mary, and I decided to connect our rooms by tearing out the back of a closet. The plan was to make tunnels everywhere. I am not sure what happened to this ingenious plan but no matter we were having clean innocent fun. Probably the worst thing we did that year was raid the kitchen at night. Ask Sylvia as she was in charge of these adventures. This was literally as bad as we got, that year.

I was so happy during these years. I was convinced nothing could ever go bad again. I remember being so content. It was all onward and upward. The school itself was hard and a challenge. Great teachers. All women teachers, to go along with the all-girl school. To me it was like a spend the night party. Year round with mandatory study halls. I fit right in.

We were taught French by Miss Lila; English by Miss Keith, history by Mrs. Morgan just to name a few. We had an assembly every day and sports every afternoon. You were either on the purple or the white team. G0 purple! Ashley Hall under the guidance of headmistress Miss Pardue and the even temperamental Mrs. Brown watched the boarders at 'our home away from home.' I felt like I was part of one big family.

Some people called us "Trashly Ashley." They were so wrong. The girls at Ashley Hall were, in my books, the cream of the crop. We were not sent away because we were bad girls. Maybe a few were, but for the most part we were very inquisitive bright young women who loved life and learning. Learning included scholastics and life in general. It was the late 60's and early 70s. Gloria Steinberg had launched the feminist revolution, which even touched the South. The Vietnam War was raging, our hormones were raging and we were living in the city where the first shot of the confederate war was shot. Talk about changes happening in our small world. We were destined to become a part of the new world, like it or not.

We studied the full spectrum of an impressive boarding school curriculum along with sewing and type writing on ancient machines for both subjects. We were a mixture of the old southern belle and the new modern woman. We wanted to be taken seriously but still expected our elders to rescue us when needed. We spoke French, read classics and studied art history along with romance novels. Smoking with permission, playing bridge in the smoking rooms or the shell house was all expected. Citadel Cadets came to see us along with the male students at our brother school Porter Gaud. That did not keep our wandering eyes from looking for the Charleston born males. They were usually older and it did not matter if they lived north or south of Broad. We were eclectic girls with a passion for living life to its fullest.

Some of the hangouts we held court in were the El Cid off King Street, a cozy pub like bar with shadowy areas so as not to be seen. Big John's off East Bay was like a speakeasy where they opened the top slatted doors to see who you were before they let you enter. It was a great pool hall. Folly Beach and the Citadel Beach parties along with the locals in their beach homes at The Isle of Palms and Sullivan's Island were always good places to plant yourself on the weekends.

This freedom to roam was earned over time. Again, at first only church, the Red and White on Wednesdays were the only allowed out trip. Next we were allowed to walk down Calhoun to King Street on Saturday.

If you had decent grades you got out for a parlor date on campus or maybe even a date on Friday night. Of course you signed out and signed in. I think you had to come in by 10 pm or 11pm. I will never forget helping buddies sign and then walk up the spiral staircase. The housemothers acted suspicious but they seemed to turn their heads knowingly so we could all get to bed. They were good to us.

The years at Ashley Hall flew by. The boarding students were like a large tight knit family. After all, you literally lived with each other 24/7. When it came time to graduate it was a time of celebrating and also a time of hysterical crying. Most of us did not want to be separated. That is just how close we had become. Fortunately we were able to extend our time together by having a house party at the beach in Cherry Grove, (I covered more details of those times in my story, The Grand Strand) A close tie has kept us together for nearly 40 years in fact we have our 40th reunion sneaking up on us and I guarantee there will be a good turnout.

**Converse College:** Many females in my family attended Converse College. It was an all-girls college. My sister and many first cousins graduated from there and to top it off your Daddy's sister plus others in his family went there as well. It was a decision that was pretty much made for me, and it suited me very well. I was used to having dorm mothers, signing in and signing out plus no men in the living areas.

It was 1973 and life continued to out-do itself as far as I was concerned. I was living with other southern girls including many friends from Ashley Hall and my freshman year roommate was Nancy Coggins. Rules were strict at Converse but we did not mind. They seemed lenient to us. We got to go to fraternity parties at Wofford College where my brother had gone in the 60's. I was comfortable.

Daddy always told me to enjoy school and study what I liked so I majored in Art History and minored in French. I had planned to go to France and study at the Louvre but the love bug got me instead. I hurried up and graduated in three years to marry my first husband. We were truly too young to know what we were getting into so the marriage did not last very long. I just was too immature but you couldn't have told me that at the time. We had a huge southern wedding and Daddy always said the cost of the wedding was not proportionate to the length of the marriage. In other words he had not finished paying for the flowers.

Without telling you the whole soap opera of my life I am not sure you will understand what really happened. You already know I met your Daddy after I got my real estate license in Greenville, SC. After a while things got a little complicated so I packed up, got a divorce and moved home to Horry County. I proceeded to try and recapture my youth. It cannot be done. I started dating lots of different people, got an apartment in Myrtle Beach with Norma Campbell, and began working for granddaddy at the Ferry and life was good again.

We had a blast at the beach. I enjoyed working for Daddy and being foot loose and fancy-free. A fling here or there with Bo Bryan and then, before I knew it the love bug hit again. Your Daddy started calling me, I decided he was the one and vice versa and we got engaged to be married, got married at the Ferry and then I moved to Simpsonville.

You three showed up within the next 4 years and there you have it. That is a cliff notes version of your Daddy and my whirlwind courtship and y'alls births. We had our hands full then and now! Fast forward to 2014.

We are still not normal, as y'all well know. I think that would be dull as dishwater. You reckon there is such a thing as a normal family? I don't think so. That is what makes us all different. God planned it that way. Don't you think?

# Christy Douglas: I'm Just Me

Since this is not a resume, I want to hit the highlights of my life. I haven't won lots of awards, and I'm not famous. I'm just me.

- Born October 18, 1954, several days after Hurricane Hazel. They almost named me Hazel, and I do have hazel green eyes.

- Attended kindergarten at 5 years old at 1st Presbyterian Church, Mullins, SC. First thing they told me was "Don't color outside the lines." I think that made me a little rebellious. I was always very independent

- Elementary school-McCormick, Mullins, SC. 1st-7th grade. Loved holding offices in the student council. Practically lived with Jane Graves who lived next door to the school.

- Mullins High School. 8th and 9th grade. Back then, there were no middle schools. In 9th grade my only brother, George, died.

- Ashley Hall School for Girls –A boarding school in Charleston, SC. 10th, 11th, 12th grades-President of Sr. Class, President of Student Council

- Converse College- A girl's college. BA in Art History, minor in French, President of several classes. Graduated in 3 years to get married. Very stupid – "Do as I say, not as I did."

- Graduated Suma Cum Laude from Converse in 1975

- Married 1st husband Perrin Trotter- lived in Greenville. Secretary, salesman, and real estate salesman

- Moved home to Galivants Ferry in 1979 and worked for Pee Dee Farms Corporation (tried to re-discover youth – it cannot be done)

- Married my 2nd husband – your Daddy, David Duvall Douglas in 1982

- Lived in Simpsonville, SC – Gave birth to Christian Monroe Holliday Douglas (1983), Marjorie Russell Holliday Douglas (1985), David DuVall Douglas, Jr. (1987). Raised you three the best I could...

- Full time Mama – moved to Greenville, SC and lived at 105 Barksdale Greene

- Junior League of Greenville member. Favorite placement was at "Camp Opportunity" – a camp for abused and neglected children. You three went with me to all events with these children. It was very special.

- Community V.P. for Junior League

- Headed up a public relations effort to change the image of Jr. League in general - won a national award for "Look Again" a PSA showing diversity of this traditionally Southern group of women.

- Moved back to Galivants Ferry, SC in 1998. Work- Monroe Management our family business, farming, real estate.

- Track coach at Pee Dee Academy- (8th -12th –boys and girls). I started the team and never cut anyone. I wanted to make sure each child was able to be a part of a team.

- Head of Public Relations for Galivants Ferry Stump.

- Active in Preservation of local Galivants Ferry buildings

- Member: First Presbyterian Church of Florence, SC

- 2010, 2011,and 2012 - Mission Trip to the Amazon Rainforest

- In 2014, I was recognized at Converse College as one of the 125 outstanding alumnae for the school's 125th anniversary. My family was so proud of me! The Alumnae Association Board recognized 125 Converse graduates who demonstrated high levels of achievement and/or service in one or more of the Seven Core Values of Converse College – Excellence, Integrity, Exploration, Diversity, Respect, Community, and Progress.

- Hobbies – volunteering, hunting, fishing, golf, exercise, yoga, meditation, photography, working in yard, animal lover, travel, writing, talking to people, playing the piano.

- Look forward to more mission trips, traveling with family, playing with my husband, and spending time with my new grandson, Jack!

# David Duvall Douglas:
## Your Daddy and My Husband

I would not be writing these letters and stories if it weren't for your daddy.

He was the baby of Rosa Fair Douglas and John Thompson Douglas. Your daddy was born September 7, 1949 in Greenville, and had a brother which y'all knew well as Uncle John (an outspoken bright southern gentleman with a delightful sense of humor) and a sister y'all call Aunt Anne (the leader of the three and now grandmother extraordinaire). They all were born and raised in their mother's hometown. They were original Greenvillians.

Your daddy swept me off my feet. I was smitten from day one. I was a young real estate "lady" (as your daddy liked to call me) and I loved helping first-time homebuyers find their perfect love nests. Your daddy reminded me of *my* daddy. They were both intelligent, well-read businessmen. They could get along with anyone and treated all with due respect.

Like my father, your daddy owned his own business – a real estate and insurance enterprise called The Douglas Company, which he bought from his family after his Daddy died. I started working for his company as a licensed Realtor and that started the sparks of a complicated, exciting, fiery courtship that culminated with our marriage on April 3, 1982 in a small ceremony with close friends and family at the Galivants Ferry Baptist Church.

That was the beginning of y'all. You three were the stars in the imaginations your daddy and I had of the family we would build and raise. It didn't take us long! You three were born in a total of 45 months, less than four years after our marriage, which meant we had two cribs and a day bed, three car seats, multiple strollers and a nursing or pregnant Mama for at least five consecutive years – and you wonder why I am a little crazy.

Do y'all remember head dancing when we went on trips? You three were all strapped in and fidgety, so your daddy would turn on loud music like "Dancing on the Ceiling" and we all "head danced," bouncing your heads around in beat with the music. Aren't you glad we had y'all so close together!

Okay, now for some serious business I want to impart to you all. Holly and Russell, you have always told me you wanted to marry someone just like your daddy. You can't compare relationships. Do not do this. It will not work, 'cause everyone is different and just because I found someone who reminded me of my daddy does not mean you can. Besides, they really were not alike, but to me they were. Just remember, you can't change anyone. You best love 'em to pieces now as they are, 'cause it usually won't get better after you're married. Old habits die hard. You need to feel you can't live without them.

David, Jr., this applies to you as well. Love someone for who they are and not what you want them to be.

And remember, when you marry someone, you also marry *their* family tree — roots, trunk, branches, knots, and the bugs that live in the bark as well. It would be dull if we didn't have diverse family characters amongst us. There's no such thing as a "normal" family.

The only normal I know is the setting on my washing machine. In addition, your gene pools from both the Douglas and the Holliday families are chock full of bright eccentric people. Ain't it fun!

At this time, Holly has married Drew Schaumber and Russell has married Taylor Powell. We like both trees and all the branches on the way down.

# My Three Boo-Boos

Your granddaddy coined this phrase for y'all. He just loved to have his "three boo-boos" come to Galivants Ferry to visit him and grandma.

When I was little, one of the first Bible songs I learned was "Praise Him, Praise Him, all ye little children..." This song reminds me of how good God is to your father and me. We were blessed with three healthy children: our three boo-boos.

I can see the image of granddaddy smiling with a glint of a tear in his eyes as he welcomed you all to the 'home place.' Your grandmama called you her grand babies, but she soon started calling you her "boo-boos" too. They would tell y'all you were HOME when you were visiting the Ferry.

Your daddy and I called you many things, depending on the moment. Among the names were Hoddy Boddy (Holly), Wuddle (Russell), and Dave Dave (David Jr.). Of course, these names progressed as the three of you learned how to talk; that skill influenced what we called each other. One in particular that I remember was the name for David, Jr. The girls called him Poindexter after a cartoon scientist. This foretold events in the future, such as David Jr. making bombs and building an assortment of "contraptions." It was always interesting at the Douglas home.

I want you to know that y'all were not in fact "Boo-Boo's." We planned for each of you, and I reckon God agreed with our wishes for children. Now, I will say you all have done your share of "boo-booing," but we always loved you no matter what.

That is what makes a happy family. Unconditional love is essential. I know sometimes we hollered, ranted, raved, cried and laughed uncontrollably. We still do, and we always will. The good news is you three will always be My Three Boo-Boo's. Ask your Daddy. Y'all will always be his, too.

Now I want to remind you of some special occasions you all celebrated when you all were too young to remember. Y'all have so many times to recollect and I want to remind you of some of the highlights.

# The Douglas Family Adventures

Our family trips should be labeled adventures, not vacations.

We always had mishaps, which are funny now but were not so funny then. That being said, I want you to know that any similarities to Chevy Chase vacation movies or Robin Williams' movie *RV* are strictly accidental.

We started traveling as a family when you all were very little. I remember someone saying, "Why travel so much when they're young? " The answer was always the same. "Children might not remember these trips, but David and I are making priceless memories." Y'all will remember some, but not all, of these excursions. That is why I need to write them down before these trips disappear from all of our minds!

In addition, I want y'all to know that these fun family car trips were not always idyllic. Yes, we are and were a rambunctious group. So in order to survive, it was necessary to be prepared for the occasional rowdy rides. I had to find something to do other than throw ice on y'all to get y'all to quiet down. The tools employed to maintain our sanity included car games and singing silly songs, and of course the famous head dancing (i.e. How to dance in a car seat). So before we start down memory lane, I want to mention a few of your favorite car games:

## The Alphabet Game
Each person selects one side of the road to look for the alphabet in road signs or billboards. The first one who can call out the words that contain the letters a through z, in order, wins. Of course, there is always a second place, and honesty is imperative in this game.

## Counting Cows
Once again, each person only gets one side of the road. The object is to see how many cows you can count within a certain length of time. Each cow counts one point. If you pass a white mule, that counts for 20 points. You must lick a finger; touch the palm of the other hand quickly and then hit the palm with your fist. If you do not do this little ceremony with your hands you forfeit the twenty points for the mule. If you pass a house with a washing machine on the porch that counts for 10 points. Passing a cemetery wipes out all your points and you have to start over! This game can get a little riotous!

## State License Plates
The key to this game is counting how many states' license plates you can see. This is done better on interstates. It's amazing how this makes time pass on long trips.

**Make Up a Story**

This game is so much fun! Everyone in the car must play and it starts like this. The first person starts a story like, "One day Miss Shy went to the circus and…" The second person adds to the story: "She saw a Fat Lady riding an elephant so…" then the third person might say, "She decided to see if they would let her ride the elephant but they said she was too…" The fourth person could finish or let it keep going by adding…. "quiet so Miss Shy told them she was not quiet and she hollered at them and got her elephant ride."

This is a silly yet creative activity. You need someone like your Aunt Russell in the mix to make it really funny. Remember her story of "little drip and big drip?" Ask her to tell you the whole story. We 'bout wet our pants from laughing so hard!

**Password**

This game is based on the old television game starring the late Allen Ludden, husband of the great Betty White. Someone selects a word and then another gives clues to his partner to help them uncover the secret word. This is one of my favorites. Good practice for vocabulary.

**Head Dancing**

This is not really a game. It's more an answer to what do you do with three antsy children locked into car seats and boosters. When y'all would start whining, I would turn up the radio to a song like "Dancing on the Ceiling" and tell you all to head dance!! You danced your head and shoulders all around 'til you all were pooped. You loved this dancing in the car! Me, too.

### 

Now for those infamous songs we sang.

I must admit, I learned these from my mother, sister, and Aunt Ethel, so I'm not the only person who thinks these songs are cute. See if you can remember the words. They really did help on those long trips. Here's the list for you to pass on to more children:

- Dunderbeck's Machine
- So You Met Someone Who Set You Back on Your Feet! Goody Goody!
- John Jacob Jingleheimer Schmidt
- I was Born One Night One Morn When the Whistle goes "Toot Toot"
- Little Rabbit in the Woods
- Jenny Made Her Mind Up
- Wee Sing Silly Songs.

I hope these games and songs have ignited some happy memories. These are just a few you can teach your children. They are interactive, and talking with one another is better sometimes than playing on an iPad, GameBoy or iPhone. Shoot, we didn't have these types of paraphernalia when y'all were growing up. We had to make up new games sometimes, and that is just as good for your mind as seclusion with a computer. Plus, you get to learn how to get along with others in different ways.

### ###

Now, here are the stories of some of our trips to finish jogging your memories. I'm going to try to highlight them. Y'all just might have to fill in some gaps!

### Christmas in Galivants Ferry

On the first trips, we packed into our huge blue and white Suburban wagon with everything we owned in order to move from Greenville, South Carolina to the Ferry for about a month every Christmas season. We were only able to do this because we spent every Thanksgiving with the Douglas' in Greenville. We have many happy memories with that whole crowd as well but I am going to focus on the trips outside of our own backyard.

Going to Galivants Ferry for Christmas was always a blast. You can say I am spoiled since I have never, ever had a Christmas any place other than 'home'. Getting there was a hassle, but the drives down were all memorable as we sang carols all the way.

Do y'all remember Granddaddy picking up the youngest of you, knocking on the living room door, and saying loudly, "Santa Claus! Are you still in there?" After you all got too big to pick up, he would pick up a kitty cat and carry it into the living room, where Santa had slid down the chimney. Tradition is tradition, which is why we always carry a cat into our Santa room today.

The Christmas that stands out the most in my mind was the year it actually snowed Christmas Eve and we, including Mama and Daddy, had our very first white Christmas! Of course, we repeated the white Christmas in 2010 — but y'all were older then.

## Sapphire Valley, North Carolina

This time with the Douglas family during the week of July 4th holds more wonderful gaggles of memories. Rosa, also known as Gano, your other grandmama, loved having her family gather in her mountain condo. Likewise, we loved spending time with your Daddy's siblings and their families. Of course, Uncle John, his wife Taffy and your cousins Katie and Rosa lived in Greenville, so we saw them quite a bit for Uncle John's pancake "eat all you can breakfasts even if it's 2 o'clock in the afternoon feasts."

We did not get to see his sister Anne Hart and her husband Bob or their children Daniel, Douglas and Anne Fair as much, so the annual July vacation with them was extra special. We had the most fun playing Scrabble, swimming in the lake, sliding down rocks into cool mountain springs, rock hunting and rafting down rapids.

The height of those times together was the actual July 4th day. There was always an all day festival of water games, lake bubble slides, picnics and the evening fireworks with a fantastic musical group of some sort. Of course, we always tended to lose one of you kids in the crowd but we found you in time to straggle up the mountain hills back to Gano' condo. It was always a jam-packed schedule for all of us – guaranteed prime family fun.

## The Russell Round Up

This was and still is our family reunion with the Russell side of the family, which is your grandmama's family. It was always held at the Myrtle Beach house.

This large beautified oceanfront home was the scene of many memories, and the Round Up was and still is the most colorful. We always had this huge country meal on Friday, thanks to all, but especially because Jenny Lou was there to produce her famous "fix one more plate full of servings but save room for the thousand-layer chocolate cake that Mrs. Johnson made for us."

Of course, many other famous desserts were provided and the country breakfasts were huge and famous. I wonder how we were able to actually go out and play golf after eating all these scrumptious meals. We did and the captains' choice teams were always interestingly put together. I never have been on the winning team.

On the Saturday nights we went out to eat at the Sea Captains house or some other family seafood restaurant. We really bonded well at those reunions. I want you all to remember family reunions are important. Promise me you three will continue The Russell Round Up…Okay?

## Disney World

Disney World trips were always wonderful. They were magical. We wanted to save money, so we drove all the way to Florida and stayed outside of the Magic Kingdom several times. Then we gave in when Aunt Russell went with us and talked us into flying and staying inside the park. As always, the five of us packed into one room. It was cozy and so great being so close to The Magic Kingdom! Even Grandmama and Granddaddy went with us on another visit.

I will never forget your Granddaddy. He did not want to get in a wheel chair but when he found out you could be first in line in the parks that made him glad to be the wheelchair recipient. He always had a child or two pushing him around. He loved it. Having them join us was special.

One of the best memories at Disney World was little Russell's birthday party in Cinderella's castle. I still do not know how they found Cinderella for this special occasion. Again, it was just magical. Other memories were you kids getting all the autographs of Mickey, Minnie and Goofy among others. We still have the autograph books. I need to show them to you. That will certainly jiggle your memories.

## New York City

We have been to The Big Apple several times. No trip there can beat the memory of visiting the World Trade Center and eating in Windows of the World, the restaurant at the top of one of the twin towers. Amazing indescribable images remain in my mind. God Bless all who have been affected by the tragedy of the losses from the demise of those buildings and the people in them. We must count our blessings.

On a lighter note, visiting the Statue of Liberty and climbing to the top, tours on the big Red Bus Line and the plays enjoyed on Broadway were and are continuous reasons to visit this multi-faceted city.

## Trips Around the U.S.A.

They don't call us the "Water Bug Family" for nothing. We have been so fortunate to have traveled to many places in the good old United States of America. I cannot go into details of all the trips, but I do want to list some of them. I think you will remember most of these anyway.

**Washington, DC**
All of the Smithsonian museum tours led by your sweet daddy. The air and space museum was your favorite plus seeing items like the ruby slippers from The Wizard of Oz.

**Amish Country**
Remember the driving tour your daddy had us take? Your daddy was famous for finding the driving historical trip tapes for cars. Most of us really just wanted to hang out in nearby Hershey, Pa. where the smell of fresh chocolate permeated the atmosphere! We did both. Yummy.

**Paradise Ranch, Wyoming**
What a great place for families. Do you recall the talent contest? David Jr. at age 4 told his joke which goes like this: "How does a farmer count his cows? With a 'COW-culator'. He got an honorable mention and a few chuckles. We all got our own horse for a week, you learned songs about 'scat', and we had our own rodeo! I think we ought to go back there again!

**Salmon River, Idaho**
When we landed in Boise, the power grid of the west went ker-plunk. To this day, our friends from South Carolina, especially the Timmons, think it was because the Douglas "water bugs" descended on Idaho.

We had to take a tiny plane from Boise into the Salmon area wilderness, and then ride a bus for an hour 'til we got to the river launching area. We chose between using kayaks, fun-yaks, canoes or a huge raft. This trip down the north fork of the Salmon River was super. Having someone put up our tents and cook scrumptious meals was right down our ally. That was our kind of camping, huh?

**The Big RV Trip Out West**
A month in a RV is a long time with a family of five. So many incredible memories stand out: visiting Zion, the Grand Canyon, the Redwood Forest, Bryce Canyon, Canyon de Chelly, Monument Valley, Grand Tetons, the Petrified Forest…the list goes on and on. You can do a lot in a month!

The one thing we all learned is RV frequenters have their own language. Will you ever forget discovering the need for "blue crystals" for the septic system? Your daddy and little David did a good job handling that part of mechanics for the trip. Like in the movie, *RV*, they did a great job learning how to drain the sewer tank with a special large snake like hose.

We learned a lot on that trip by stepping outside our/my comfort zone, including how to enjoy jumping into freezing water because we were so hot we could not breathe, how to enjoy having three dirty children and living in a constantly messy RV, and how to finally enjoy the site of my children half naked playing in the fire ashes. We didn't call little David Smut Nose for nothing.

Driving across Death Valley was interesting, too, since we were told not to drive through this treacherous area. During the day, your tires could melt. At night, the wind could blow you off the road.

We survived this trip because all our friends in Greenville prayed for us. They knew we did not follow directions very well plus we were indeed the Water Bug Family, which meant we never, ever, went in a straight line. Wandering off beaten paths was our specialty.

Oh, I forgot to mention your most favorite place and your father's...Craters of the Moon. I told your father you three wanted to have another trip there as a surprise one day! Just teasing!

## Cruises
We started going on these when puberty started. At least you were contained on a ship. The best one was celebrating my Mama and Daddy's 50th wedding anniversary. That was a special week being with them and Aunt Russell. It was one of those huge ships where you stayed lost the whole cruise, but at least we knew or hoped you wouldn't jump off. I don't think we will do that again. It wasn't a private beach.

## St. Lucia
This was the all-inclusive family resort where you wore a colored band on your wrist to prove you were a guest. Holly, you learned how to Scuba Dive there and wore your first bikini. It was the first and last island trip we took. Hormones were rampant.

## Eastern Europe
This was a whirlwind trip through Hungary, Germany, the Republic of Czech, Austria, Poland, Slovakia and Switzerland. We even had a side trip to Lithuania to get our passports stamped. In the next chapter, I go into detail about our jaunt in Budapest while traveling with little Russell's ballet troupe.

Russell, you remember this trip was actually a ballet trip with Barbra Selvy's Dance School and the whole family joined you and all the other ballerinas. Your Daddy was the only male adult, and David Jr. was one of two younger boys on this bus trip. That in itself made the voyage even more interesting. Your Daddy was almost a bell cap for the young women. It wasn't easy for him to take directions from twenty ballerinas. He was happy, but there came a breaking point. He wanted to be the man in charge.

Several other great recollections include: Not being able to take a photograph in McDonalds in Slovakia (the men with machine guns thought we might steal the restaurant idea we supposed); driving like we were in a race car on the German autobahn; running into first cousins at a Rick Steves' suggested hotel in Strasburg; getting lost on a 'foggy no rails Swiss mountain pass' in our car; our panicky unguided Alps hiking trip; and the Swiss cows with bells larger than their heads.

It's funny what you remember on trips. I want to thank all our friends for praying for us. We finally made it across the shortcut through the unmarked Alps mountain pass at night to a fancy Grendlewald Hotel and then back home in one piece.

But I think we will always laugh hardest when one of us says "Budapest! Budapest!" to the other. It's one of our best inside jokes.

Here is the story of that infamous Douglas family adventure. One night, your Daddy told us: "Get ready for an adventure. We are going on a cruise down the Danube in Budapest!" It was already late, but the sun had not set, so he figured we had plenty of time to find the port for the boat on the Danube.

Picture this: your daddy in charge, followed by second-in-command David Jr., his only other male figure, stomping out into the streets of Budapest headed to the city trains. We were three women following in a dutiful row behind our leaders. Girls, do you remember we kept saying that we were going the wrong way? Do you remember we were totally ignored? Instead we went the wrong way on the wrong train. Your Daddy had put little David in charge of monitoring the train map in his hands with the directions in the train.

After several stops, it was apparent we were headed in the wrong direction towards the countryside beyond Budapest. David Jr. announced, "Daddy, there is nothing on this map in my hand that matches that map up there."

A bilingual student laughed and told us, "You are on the wrong train; Get off at the next stop! Ha-ha!"

I would have enjoyed being right if we had not have been lost. We quickly grabbed our stuff including all of our passports and valuables (we were checking out the next morning), hopped out quickly, the train doors swiftly closed and there we were…in the middle of Budapest countryside on an empty train platform, with the sun setting, and howling critters in the distance. I could see the headlines in the paper:

*5 UNSEASONED AMERICAN TOURISTS STRIPPED OF ALL THEIR GOODS AND LEFT IN THE MIDDLE OF NOWHERE WITH NO PROOF OF IDENTITY NOR MONEY*

We all grew very nervous, but tried not to get too upset. Surely, there had to be a way back to our hotel.

About that time, a young boy on a bicycle came up to the platform to see when the next train would be coming. We were so happy to see another person that we scared him off with our panicky inquiries. As he quickly rode away, some of us started to tear up. What now?

Then Russell saw a glint of light in the distance. We all went towards it. Thank goodness it was an innkeeper sweeping up and preparing to close. David Sr. told me to go talk to him in sign language.

Off I went to communicate in sign language. When my exclamation of "Budapest, Budapest! Choo-choo!" got me a shake of the head – as in 'no' – I tried something else.

"Taxi! Taxi! Budapest, Budapest!" I shouted. I waved my arms trying to make the words seem more animated.

"Ahhh," he said and handed me the phone.

"No, not me!" I pointed at myself, then at him, and handed him the phone.

"Ahhh," he said again and called us a taxi.

At that point, it looked like everything was going to be fine, thanks to hand language and lots of smiles. We stayed there drinking homemade wine out of vats and orange soda, the best wine I have ever had. Soon the taxi came, and we got back to our hotel just in time to start loading up the buses again for our next leg of the trip.

We never did tell any of the others on the trip about our adventures. We wanted to protect the men. I think your Daddy planned an event like that so you three would be ready to move anywhere, so long as you could survive this trip and get back on American soil.

Of course, there were many more close calls on this magnificent trip. It really was a great way to spend the last few weeks prior to the Big move to the Ferry. It got everyone's mind off reality of what was about to happen to our family.

## Africa
You remember this trip for sure. Our guide, Gary Tonks, picked us up in Elizabethtown, South Africa. He was the best, coolest guide we have ever had. We went from South Africa to Botswana, Zambia and Zimbabwe before ending in Cape Town. This trip opened our eyes as to how blessed we are. We visited Soweto and Robbens Island, where Nelson Mandela lived and was imprisoned. We actually had professional hunter guides, and the hunts were true big-game hunting.

The stay in Zambia showed us how woman were positioned in society in parts of Africa. One particular night is bound to be imprinted in your memories. Girls, remember when we tried to teach the women in Zambia how to stand up for themselves? I still can't believe we sat on the ground 'beneath' the men during supper. Of course the women did all the cooking, including dried minnows, a delicacy, which we all tasted. After dinner, we all dressed in beautiful scarves and we taught each other traditional dancing. Flying over Victoria Falls in a helicopter was thrilling, too, but the most hazardous thing our family did was watch, and go along with, David Jr. and Gairy, as they bungee jumped off the Victoria Falls bridge. What were we thinking?

## The Infamous Trip to Italy
We hopped aboard a Perillo tour bus and took a wild and wooly trip through Italy. But our stop in Venice took the cake for sure. Those gondoliers were so cute, but their fingers were sticky and they loved young American women! The young Italian and Venetian women loved cute American boys, too.

We lost all three of you for an entire night. Your father went out on the streets of Venice searching for y'all and left me at our hotel praying and mashing my teeth. You three finally showed up at dawn in time to move to the next town. All of you were teenagers and we swore we would never, ever take y'all on a trip again.

## The Galapagos

Ok…we did take you all on another trip. We flew into Ecuador and then to the Galapagos Islands, a wonder world of unique animals and critters. We stayed on a small ship with about a hundred people, a perfect size for getting to know others. It was a wonderful adventure of photography and swimming with penguins.

The blue-footed Boobies were just one of the very unique and rare critters we were able to admire on this fascinating trip. Y'all earned the rights to future family vacations. It appeared you were growing up. We ended the trip with an all-day drive across the Andes, back in Equidor to a part of the Amazon. We bonded on this trip in a good way.

## Istanbul and the Black Sea Voyage

Your Daddy picked this trip out all on his own. He then found suggested reading for each of us, so we could understand this part of the world. This was going to be an educational trip. What we did not know was the other guests on the ship were from Ivy League Schools. It was a reunion for Harvard, Brown and other prestigious colleges. And then there was us.

They handed out a list of people and where they were from. We were listed as the Douglas Family from Aynor, South Carolina. I told them we represented UCLA (aka upper Conway and lower Aynor). It really was fun because the people were so interesting, and traveling from port to port in the Black Sea was exciting. We were not very knowledgeable about our surroundings, but we certainly learned a whole lot. Russell, do you remember asking for Chinese restaurants when we went to the Asian side of Istanbul?

This period of time was the same time that Russia was bombing Georgia. We actually saw the Russian ship passing in front of us headed to Georgia. That kept us from stopping there for sure. (More praying going on at home)

The Ukraine, Bulgaria, Yalta, Istanbul and all the stops made us count our blessings. The people were so friendly and appeared very happy, but it made us appreciate the USA. On the way to the airport, the roads were blocked off as the President of Iran was now in Istanbul. We actually made it to the airport and boarded the last departing plane. The air traffic was put on hold till the Iranian leader returned to Teheran. We had fun but it was nice flying home.

### ###

These are all the family trips I can remember, kids. We certainly have been blessed and appreciate being able to see other parts of our nation and the world. I want to give your Daddy credit for 99% of these adventures. They say he and I have ants in our pants; that is an accurate description. We hope we have instilled in y'all a sense of wanderlust and a continued curiosity about this big world we live in.

Traveling is fun, educational, and an eye opener to other cultures. These travels have led me to want to write my book called *Familiar Faces*. We must respect others all over the world and be open-minded about other ways and customs. We all come into this world the same. It's what we do with our lives that makes the difference. You can read more about this in my next book, so right now, I just want you to contemplate the many places you have been privileged to visit. What memories stand out in your minds? What questions do you have for the people you have met? How have these travels affected your way of thinking? Have fun reminiscing. I certainly have.

# The Big Move: City Comes to the Country

August 1998: We *almost* moved from Greenville to Galivants Ferry.

We had said all our goodbyes, removed all of y'alls names from the roster at Christ Church Episcopal School, resigned from any duties and literally packed up and attempted to move to the country from the city. Tears aplenty, anger eruptions as predictable as Old Faithful, dirty looks, sassy remarks and a sad drive accompanied us on the forever trek to the Ferry.

What we didn't know is there would be no room in the big white house for us. Yep, you heard me right. Your grandparents loved us plenty, but when we couldn't find suitable housing close by and the only place for us to live was with them, something unbelievable happened. They told us, "NO, you cannot live with us. Period."

So, we packed back up, put our tails between our legs and snuck back to Greenville, re-enrolled you in school and resumed all our other duties that accompany life in a big city. We acted like nothing happened. I will never forget the barrage of "I thought you all moved!" "What happened to your move?" It was endless till after a couple of weeks, when new news replaced our ill-fated stab at moving to the Lowcountry of South Carolina.

A year passed uneventfully as we fixed up the "Big Playhouse" at the Ferry (literally a building in which we used to play, but in actuality, it was the kitchen for the original old home place). Daddy was glad we were moving home again but spending money on this old building drove him nuts. Daddy was tight as a tick on some things. I reckon it was 'cause he grew up during the Depression. At any rate, the revitalization of this fine old dilapidated building finally concluded and it was time to try the move once more.

You kids were holding out that we had changed our minds. Nope. Your daddy had put your names on the waiting list for Pee Dee Academy in Mullins, South Carolina and you got in. It was his idea, not mine. I give him full credit. Chances are, I would have stayed in Greenville, but he was determined it was the best thing for you all to move and get to know the other side of your family. He also knew you would love the country versus the city.

After we got home from our Eastern Europe trip in one piece, we packed up, moved to Galivants Ferry the next day and you three went to a new school the following day. There was no sense spreading out the misery. Just jump in headfirst. That is what we did by moving in the big playhouse. All was great – except y'all did not speak to your Daddy or me for months as I recall, and you paid us back in many ways, which I will keep secret. Suffice it to say, the first couple of years were tough, but y'all finally got used to this new way of life and I think you three are now happy that we moved. Right? Maybe?

From your father's and my point of view, it was the right decision. You were 9, 11, and 13, tender ages for sure. I still think that getting to know your grandfather and grandmother, plus experiencing a brand new life, was well worth all the pain. You all look happy as clams now and you have friends all over the state of South Carolina. There is one thing you need to know. It was all your Daddy's idea to move. So he truly gets all the credit.

I was sure that you were being brought to live in Galivants Ferry to experience the same kind of childhood I had experienced. Boy, was I wrong! Your Aunt Russell warned me: "Christy, it's not the same. You are going to have a hard time moving those children. You might have loved climbing trees, catching tadpoles, and riding by yourself each afternoon, but your children will be like fish out of water."

She was right. Not only did you all have a tough time, but the tree house wasn't there, the tadpole slew had dried up, the barns and other structures were being torn down, and the life I knew was rapidly disappearing! I had wanted to introduce to the South I knew. I wanted you to love the Ferry, play in the fields, climb the trees, shoot BB guns, roller-skate on the ancient tennis courts, make mud pies with your cousins, explore the old buildings (the ones that had not been torn down) and ride horses through the bone yard. It seemed like a sure thing to me. Again, I was wrong. Things had changed. But it drove me to a new passion: I just had to stop the bulldozers and find a reason to save The South I Knew.

I know you didn't plan to be a part of this new passion of mine, but you are. Thank you for moving to the home place. Thank you for making me realize I cannot reinvent the past. The good news is we can preserve and spread the love for the way of life I recall. It's funny how God always has plans for us that we had no idea about. He surprises us all the time.

You all are part of the fifth generation of Hollidays to live in Galivants Ferry. That is special. Join me in carrying on traditions here in the country. You might not continue to live here, but I promise you will always be *home* when you come back. I love you all and thank you for being so adaptable. I know it wasn't easy, but it helped make y'all who you are today.

# PART VI
## Remnants of the South I Knew

# Disappearing Contraptions

I have already told y'all the story of why I started writing down these recollections and taking photographs.

The reasons still stand firm, but the base of the platform has widened. It not only includes Southern things (though most are Southern), but memorabilia that are disappearing due to "progress" and just plain ol' changing times.

Included in this book are some of the photographs I have learned to treasure due to the fact that so many of my subjects have fallen down or disappeared, even in the last few years. We are in some ways a "throw-it-all-away" society. I specifically mean old buildings full of history. If only these structures could talk. Imagine what they could tell us. No, you can't hang on to all old structures and stuff, but I am making a stab at saving what I can. Some of the disappearing contraptions are smaller than buildings, yet were a large part of lifestyles back when. I mean even back to my earlier years, not to mention those before me.

The bottom line is this: part of my love letters to y'all includes a wrap up of details or photographs not covered in the first part of my recollections. They just didn't fit in properly. Keep these photos and lists as reference to document in a small way how our lives and the world around us are continually evolving. Maybe you can start documenting your lives for your own future family members. Better start now, 'cause it ain't easy.

# Sharing Memories

Writing about The South I Knew is getting more fun by the minute! Y'all know a lot about Paul Owens, but you don't know much about Glenda, his wife. Glenda has told me stories lately about working in tobacco fields, vegetable gardening, hog killing times, river traditions on the black rivers of the Little Pee Dee, and some unbelievable recipes that only a true southerner could possibly know about!

This has gotten my creative juices moving even more. Preserving these incredible memories of times past is so important to me and to the world. The way of life has changed around here, like everywhere else in the world. That is normal, right? Some of it is for the good, and some for the bad, but none of us can stop it. So, we have to preserve it. The only way to do this is to write it down, talk about it, tell your children, and fill out the family Bible (or family tree).

How many times have you said to yourself, "I wish I had written that down or I wish my granddaddy or great aunt, etc. had told me about this or that?" It is our duty to make sure we preserve the times when tobacco was king, a kind word to a stranger was normal, a wave and a smile to folks you pass on the road was the thing you just did – without thinking twice about it! Also, there were many more activities, gestures, sayings, and occupations during yesteryear. River baptisms, family gatherings at the bridge (where the ferry was), tall tale stories of fishin' or just playing on the river, or cleaning up after working in the summer heat... your memories of times gone by is important.

It gets me all riled up just thinking about how much there is to pass on to future generations. I am not a historian, for sure. I am working from memories and the memories of others. Like other societies in faraway states or countries, if we don't document it, all will be lost.

Speaking of one of those memories, remember how I mentioned Glenda Owens at the beginning of this piece? Now I will give her center stage for a moment with a story of her own. Take it away, Glenda!

# Hog Killin' Time
## As told by Glenda Owens

*Author's Note: If your stomach is a little queasy, read Glenda's story later!*

Back when I was a young girl, we had to help kill hogs.

My dad would always start the night before by getting the pit ready for the fire and setting the vat up. A vat was a large barrel cut in half to put water in. He would get up early the next morning and start the fire so the water would be hot to put the hog in so we could scrape the hair off the hog. When the water got hot he would take his .22 rifle and go shoot the hog and cut his throat so he would bleed out. Then he would drag the hog over to the vat and roll him in the hot water. We would all have sharp knives, so when the hog came out of the water, we would start scraping the hair off. This hair was very coarse and hard to get off.

After we got the hair off, it was time to gut the hog. Mom would always have pans ready to put the liver, lights (lungs of the hog), intestines or chitlins in. Then Mom, my sister and I would have to go to the field beside the house and clean the chitlins. Mom would always cut the intestines about two to three feet in length. She would run her hand down the outside of the casing to clean the stuff out of it. Then we would have to pour water through the casing until it was clean. She would always wash them five to six times. We were always far away from the house, so we had to carry water in a bucket to where we were working. After we got through cleaning the chitlins outside, Mom would take them in the house and wash them again and again. She would use a stick to turn them inside out to clean them some more.

While we were cleaning the chitlins, Dad and my brother would be cutting up the hog into quarters and trimming the fat. The fat would go into a big pile to be cut up to make cracklings, but first, we would use salt to rub down the ham and shoulders to put in the smoke house to cure. Dad would cut the back up into pork chop. They would keep the pig's feet to make "pickled pig feet" and the head, which was used to make "hog head cheese." (See recipe below).

After all the meat was put up, we would start cutting up the fat into about three to four inch stripes to cook crackling. The fat was put in a large case iron pot over a fire of gas cooker. We had to stir the fat so it would not burn or scorch to the bottom of the pot. Once the fat started to heat up, it would turn into oil. You would cook the fat until it was all dried up and all you had left was a crunchy piece of skin. Then you would remove the oil from the fire and let it cool. It was then poured into large buckets and use to cook with. That was how you made lard. You saved everything.

Believe me or not: it is all delicious. Try the recipes out for yourselves. This one has been a family recipe for three generations.

## Hoghead Cheese (Souse meat)

- one large hog head
- apple cider vingar
- one large onion (chopped)
- black pepper
- salt
- red pepper
- sage

*Split hog head in half (remove hog brains and eyes) put in large pot and boil until tender. Remove all meat from bones, grind or mash fine. Add sage, red pepper, chopped onion, black pepper and salt to taste. Pour into a large pan, press it down to remove all air. Allow to chill in the refrigerator overnight.*

## Grandma Gracie's Pickled Pigs Feet

- 3 1/4 lbs. pigs feet
- Cold water
- 2/3 c. white vinegar
- 6 tbsp. sugar
- 1 1/2 tbsp. salt
- 1 tsp. pickling spice
- 5 pepper kernels

*Place clean pigs feet into 4 quart pot. Cover with cold water; bring to boil Simmer until meat is fairly tender. Cool for 8 to 10 hours. Drain, reserving liquid and place meat into jars. Combine 2 1/4 cups of liquid and remaining ingredients. Bring to boil and simmer for a few minutes. Pour over pig's feet. Cool and refrigerate. Serve cold.*

*Try it! You just might like it!*

# Memories from a Lowcountry Game Warden
## As told by Ben Moise

Here is another recollection by my good friend Ben Moise. Ben is a retired game warden, and a fabulous outdoor cook who specializes in oyster roasts and Frogmore Stew. He is also the author of *Ramblings of a Low-Country Game Warden: A Memoir* and *A Southern Sportsman: The Hunting Memoirs of Henry Edwards Davis)*. Ben and his lovely wife, Anne, live in downtown Charleston.

"I remember (hog killing time) well at my grandparents' farm when I was growing up in Bishopville. My grandfather, James Edmund McCutchen shot them right in the top of the forehead, then they were immediately drug over to a cedar log rack with a pulley.

The hog was pulled up hanging by his hind legs and his throat cut. All the hands would be standing around with cups and jars to receive the fresh blood, which, to our amazement, they would drink right down and smack their lips. Then they would lower that hog in a huge cauldron of water to scald and hoist it up again where they would begin scrapping off the hair and outer dark layer of skin.

When they finished, it would take on a white appearance. Then it would be gutted and various pieces-parts parceled out to the hands. Out of the innards, Grandfather would save only the liver for making puddin'. That hog would be then put on a long table and cut up as Glenda described, bacon and hams to the smoke house, some cut up to go for making sausage, fat to the rendering pot.

I noticed various savory parts would be sitting around on rocks around the fires, 'dropped' there by the hands for a quick snack amidst all the labor. The hog killin' in Rowesville occurred at Norman Hughes's Hog Parlor where a squealin' pig would go from dead to sausage in a millisecond. "Uncle Norman" was Ernestine's uncle and when a hog killing was called, everyone in the countryside would attend and everybody had something to do. When the work was done, Laddie would serve the crowd one of his legendary BBQ's, the hash made from boiling down the hog's heads and a couple of cow tongues. Talk about GOOD!"

# Working in Tobacco

Recently, Glenda Owens vividly described what it was like to work in tobacco.

I learned more than I ever knew about this process. I'd always heard how grueling it could be, but not till she explained it to me did I understand. I promise all story comes straight from her mouth and memories. You can't make up stories like this.

"We all would work in the fields in the summertime; my mom, my sister, Sherry, and my brother, Barry. My youngest brother, Gary, was too young to work so he just played around in the dirt all day. We would have to get up early around 6 AM. Get breakfast and be ready to go by 7 AM. to start working.

"We worked with the Vaught family. They would pick us up and head to the tobacco beds. We would go pull plants to set them out in the fields. We would pull plants for about 2 1/2 to 3 hours. Enough that would last all day. Then we would head to the field to start settin' out the plants on the tobacco setter. Even if you were too young to work, you were still up and at the fields, playing at the end of the rows or getting in trouble. After we got through settin' the tobacco out, we waited a couple of weeks 'til the tobacco grew. So did the weeds.

Then we had another job hoeing the weeds out of the tobacco or pulling them up by hand if they were too close to the plant. When the plants got so big they would "lay them by" – plowing the fields and throwing the dirt around the tobacco. Then we would have to uncover the plants if the dirt got on 'em. We kept pullin' weeds, and hoeing till the tobacco got big enough to shade the weeds and grass out. But somehow, the morning glories would manage to keep growing. They would wrap around the tobacco stalk and we would have to pull them out. 'Make sure you get the roots or they will come back!' yelled the grown-ups. There was always something to do in the tobacco field.

"Then it was time to sucker and top (pinch the suckers and pop the flower off the top). We always wanted the rows with the tops because it was easy to just pop out the tops. But the suckers were all the way down the stalk, between the stalk and the leaf. We would go from one field to the next until we got all the suckers out (over and over again) 'til it was time to harvest. This was not a clean job. Your hands were always sticky and dirty. One thing you did get out there was a tan, a farmer's tan.

"We would start to harvest the tobacco when it turned from dark green to a light yellow-green. You would crop the tobacco from the bottom up, just a few leaves at a time. I remember a few times cropping on foot, but by the time I was working in the fields, we had machines that did the job for us. We did help Daniel Johnson when the Vaughts got through. Where you rode the harvester, someone would crop the tobacco and hand it to you, then would string it up on the stick. When you got through with that stick, you would yell, "Stick!" Someone would get that full stick of tobacco and you would start another one. They would put these sticks of tobacco on a trailer and take them to the barn to be hanged and ready to be cured.

"We went from cropping by hand to machine cropping, from stick barns to bulk barns. It seemed to get a little easier, but it was still hard work. When the tobacco was cured, you would unload the barn, taking the cured tobacco off the sticks, racks or boxes and putting them in a packer that was set on top of a tobacco sheet. Someone would walk inside the packer and pack it down. Then the tobacco sheets would get tied up and put to the side 'til the barn was unloaded. They would put this sheet of tobacco in the pack house until it was time to go to the market in Mullins where it was auctioned off!

"Outside of hard work, there was a lot of horseplay, breaks with the soda and tobacco crackers, plus we were able pay book fees and get new clothes for school."

Glenda is, without a doubt, one of the hardest workers I know. She can do anything, including any kind of tractor work. You name it, she can do it, but she swears she will never EVER crop or sucker tobacco anymore!

# My Favorite Southern Sayings

- Going around your elbow to get to your thumb
- Running around like a chicken with their heads cut off
- Bless yo' soul
- Miss Christy or Mr. David
- What y'all doing?
- Yes Siree Bob
- Set down for a spell
- Take a load off
- Playin it by the ears
- Pert' near
- I reckon
- Y'all
- Bless you
- Beer, Bullets, and Bait
- I love you a bushel and a peck
- Carter's got pills
- Keep your ducks in a row
- Yo' neck of the woods
- Picture shows
- Pe` can
- Toma` toes
- Nu yonder
- 'Bout to swoon!

# PART VII
## Afterthoughts

# Wisdom from Your Mother

These are some things that I have learned from my walks with God and the dogs. I want you three to hold onto these things.

- We are all the same and at the same time all different.

- Do unto others, as you would have them do unto you. Always remember the 'Golden Rule.'

- Do as I say, not as I do.

- We must be peacemakers but not wimps.

- Believe in miracles and expect them when it is in God's Will.
  Sometimes God says, "YES."
  Sometimes God says, "NO."
  "Other times He says not now.
  Remember that it is not all about you.

- Remember *The Four Agreements* by Miguel Ruiz:
  1. **Be Impeccable with your Word:** Speak with integrity. Say only what you mean. Avoid using the Word to speak against yourself or to gossip about others. Use the power of your Word in the direction of truth and love.

  2. **Don't Take Anything Personally**: Nothing others do is because of you. What others say and do is a projection of their own reality, their own dream. When you are immune to the opinions and actions of others, you won't be the victim of needless suffering.

  3. **Don't Make Assumptions:** Find the courage to ask questions and to express what you really want. Communicate with others as clearly as you can to avoid misunderstandings, sadness and drama. With just this one agreement, you can completely transform your life.

  4. **Always Do Your Best:** Your best is going to change from moment to moment; it will be different when you are healthy as opposed to sick. Under any circumstance, simply do your best, and you will avoid self-judgment, self-abuse, and regret.

- Think outside the box.

- These are the first steps in your lives. Remember there is much more to come.

- You will see loved ones again so do not be sad.

- Judge not lest ye be judged. Truth be known. John 8:32 *and ye shall know the truth, and the truth shall make you free. (KJV)*

- There are many purposes for you. Big and small. You will fall many times.

- We all like sheep have gone astray.

- All things works together for the goodness of God. We might not understand it but we have to trust Him and accept His grace and forgiveness.

- Thank God we all have many chances. We sin, we sin, we do God's will and then repeat the cycle.

- Learn how to talk to God like you would talk to your best friend.

- Find a group who puts God first and be honest with them. Find support. Find a church family, we cannot live alone. Find people who are friendly to you and are not judgmental. Find a church that fits you. It's important to get to know God as soon as you can. The peace you feel permeates your whole being. Sure, it comes and goes. That's normal, but going to church is so important. You don't have to be there every time the doors open, but Sunday would be nice. Of course, you can sit in a deer stand, too. It's a great place to clear your head and talk to God.

- You do not have to do what you do not want to do.

- Do not live for others. Take care of yourself, follow your heart, do not think you have to do anything you know is wrong or you just do not like. You do not have to do stuff you know is wrong. Do not go along for the ride. You might have to form new groups of friends.

- I am sorry I did not set good enough examples for you when it came to church. I know Jesus' birthday party and counting your blessings was good.

- You all were my guinea pigs, I will do better with my grandchildren.

- It's not "My way or the highway." Be open-minded.

- Learn to set boundaries. Learn how to react, not react and when to react. Learn to put up boundaries and walk out the door.

- Take care of yourself, then God can use you in His time, not yours.

- Never lie, steal or cheat.

- Spend daily time in prayer and the Bible.

- Talk to God every day. Let it become a habit and do not be afraid to say how you feel. Ask for wisdom.

- You can't scream out when you know it's not the right time.

- Think about it. Do not rush into anything.

- Don't do anything that would be spitting on your "blanket," (AKA: What you hold in your heart)

- Honor your heritage. Protect your loved ones.

- Get rid of your EGO…

- If it's not God's will, things will eventually fall apart.

- Do things for the right reasons.

- You can start over many times if you ask for God's will to set you free. Jenny Lou said "the truth be known." And Daddy started all his meetings with, "Let us do the right thing for the right reason." Again, remember the "Golden Rule."

- Put God first. It works.

- Ask yourself: Why are your closets fuller than others? Why am I so fortunate? Why do we have more stuff or money or clothes, etc. than others? Why were we born here rather than in the Congo? God tells us to serve and love Him, so we are to share according to our "gifts" and possessions. We are to serve others less fortunate. What you give, He will reward you multiple times over Trust God about this.
- Read *The Bible* from beginning to end.

- Read *The Treasured Principle* by Randy Alcorn.

- Read *The Purpose Driven Life* by Rick Warren.

- Read *The Four Agreements* by Miguel Ruiz.

- When God opens a door, it's not open forever. Jump in and see. Listen. Hear. Feel. Touch. Hold. Pray for Wisdom. Strive for Peace. Love, Love, Love.

- I love you all so much. Listen to God and discover your talents. Follow your hearts and passions. Be good to yourselves. Then you can do for others.

# Meditation in Deer Stands

Nothin' could be better than God's Company
Just us two, sitting in a tree

Talking is easy…no fancy words
Ain't no doubt: I know I will be heard

No subject is off limit, no subject's too absurd
God doesn't judge; so talk and you'll be heard

Honesty; always the best way
He'll understand; no matter what you say

He listens to your words in addition to your heart
God knows when you need a jump-start

When the going gets tough it's easy to give in
But with God at our side we can fight all kind of sin

Often, we let our lives get bogged down with 'stuff'
Just pray God'll hear, life needn't be so tough

Before you know it, life is focused on His will
Let your ego go and your life will be fulfilled

You can't "do it" on your own accord
That's a mistake we can't afford

So give yourself to Jesus, the only Lord and Savior
He'll never leave you; you'll receive His favor.

# It's Funny How Life Goes Around in Circles

You three are just beginning to experience the circles of life.

We're born; raised and then just when you think you understand your life things change. Schools change, friends move, you move, birthdays pass, people you love pass on. In general we grow and change and so do our surroundings, thoughts, ideas and opinions. I now realize just how smart my parents' are/were. With every birthday it becomes clearer what's important and what's not. What's real and what's fake. I assume this will continue to circle as I age until I die.

My newest circle of realization is I really love Galivants Ferry more than I thought. Sure, it's tough being in the country and far from stores malls, people, restaurants and other perks that comes from being a city/town dweller. Guess how I figured this out? Yep, writing this book for y'all and really digging deep into my insides. A few hurts do pop up by doing these exercises but the good outweighs the bad. Like Denise said in her last conversation with me. "Your Daddy told me to watch out if you drink the water of the Little Pee Dee you'll never want leave." I drank the water, breathed the clean air, watched seasons come and go and my present circle has just recently become clear to me. It took a while to get over city life but I now know I can travel and visit my city friends, see the sites of other areas, travel to other lands and know that Galivants Ferry will always be Home.

One of the truest activities that have instilled these truths in my soul has been my learning to love being alone. Alone in a deer stand watching and listening to nature, smelling the crisp clean air, and becoming one with nature. Alone, jogging in a field or on a dirt road like those at the Bay Field. Alone, walking with the dogs in the field behind our house. Alone, talking to our animals. Alone, checking the eggs in the chicken yard.

I want you three to know that Alone is anything but lonely. It's like the color black. Most people think it's colorless. Lots of folks feel alone is also colorless and lonely. It's not. It depends on how you look at life. Remember, every day is a gift. Look for the silver linings. Feel the emotions around you. Be open minded to new opportunities you face. Enjoy the new people you meet and what makes them tick. Listen to life in all forms around you and be thankful for everything. Knowing that every bad thing has a purpose (which is hard to fathom).

Life is full of changes. Roll with the punches deal with discrepancies, expect hard times, love and accept love. Give and say thank you for your gifts. Every stumbling block in life is really a stepping-stone. Keep climbing as you go through your circles of life.

I'll always be with y'all even when you don't see me. It's one of the secret circles of life that I know is there even though I don't understand it yet. Call it faith.

# It's All Up to Y'all

So there you have it.

You'll never have all of historical tales and folklores but at least you have enough to whet your appetite for finding out more about your roots, kinfolks and the changing ways of life that have occurred.

Hopefully, you'll be able to see the need to adapt if any of you want to stay here and raise your children on the "homeplace." The choice will be yours. I've never forced y'all to do anything.

Life is full of choices and we are all God's children and He may have futures He's calling you to that do not include Galivants Ferry. That's OK. I want you to follow your heart, fulfill your dreams and never feel compelled or have to do anything with regards to family obligations. You each are strong young adults with minds of your own. Who you marry and what your passions are will lead you on to where you go and live throughout your future years.

Just remember: Your family and roots in Galivants Ferry will always be here if you ever want to return to our "home place." It might even be one or several of your children. You can pass on these stories to them and when you visit us they can build tree houses in the magnolia trees, pick grapes, figs, and pecans, hunt, fish in the Little Pee Dee River, and play with their cousins like I did. Being a country girl/boy is fun.

It's good to visit the city, but ain't no place like home.

I love you always,
Mama

# About the Author

Christian Monroe Holliday Douglas was born in Galivants Ferry, South Carolina into the fourth generation of the Holliday family.

After living for a time in Greenville, South Carolina, Christy, her husband, David, and their three children – Holly, Russell, and David Jr. – returned to Galivants Ferry in 1998. Since then, Christy has been amassing stories and photographs that tell the history of the South through its people and her memories, compiling them into this book of love letters to her children.

When not writing, Christy spends her time taking photographs and tending her backyard menagerie of cats, dogs, chickens, turkeys, and peacocks. This is her first book.

Made in the USA
Lexington, KY
18 May 2014